STREET GUY

A US Secret Service Undercover Operator

THOMAS J. FARRELL

NEWMAN SPRINGS PUBLISHING
320 Broad Street
Red Bank, NJ 07701

First originally published by Newman Springs Publishing 2021

Artist Cover credit: Ericaetcetera

ISBN 978-1-63881-095-7 (Paperback)
ISBN 978-1-63881-096-4 (Digital)

Printed in the United States of America

To my wife, Christina, the most selfless and
loving partner a man could ask for

INTRODUCTION

T he United States Secret Service was established on July 5, 1865. It was formed to investigate and prosecute the counterfeiting of currency, which plagued the country during the Civil War. Secret Service did not officially protect the president and other officials until the assassination of President McKinley in 1901.

Today, Secret Service is known as the premier protective agency in the world. The men and women who surround the president, vice president, and other officials with their dark suits, sunglasses, and radio earpieces are very visible to the public and are the face of the agency. Less publicized but equally important are the agents who conduct the criminal investigative responsibilities of Secret Service.

Recently, books have been written by retired agents detailing their experiences in protective details. Some were tabloid-like in nature meant to embarrass the agency and political leaders, and others were genuinely written to express the historical significance of the agents' experiences. However, few books have been written detailing an agent's experience conducting criminal investigations and undercover operations.

This book is one agent's story of Secret Service investigative and undercover work during the 1980s and 1990s, which was the heyday of Secret Service criminal investigative activity. I am proud to say that I was a special agent with Secret Service for over twenty years, retiring in 2003 as a special agent in charge of the Special Services Division, Washington, DC.

Secret Service is a unique law enforcement agency because of its protective and investigative responsibilities. On any given day, I may be working an undercover assignment with the Gambino family in Brooklyn; and the next day, I could be working a protective assignment with the Bush family in Kennebunkport, Maine. No other law enforcement agency offered such diverse responsibilities and stark contrasts in assignments.

I would not trade my experiences with Secret Service for any other law enforcement career. Secret Service afforded me the opportunity to travel the world on protective and investigative assignments. I visited forty-five foreign countries, and I have met presidents, distinguished world leaders, and celebrities and witnessed major historical events. I worked extensive undercover assignments, both domestic and foreign, and worked undercover assignments with some of the most notorious Mafia members in New York.

As a Secret Service agent, there was always somewhere to travel or some undercover deal to put together. Work was not mundane. If you needed a break from investigative work, there was always travel for protective assignments. Personally, I never needed a break from investigations and enjoyed being on the street trying to put deals together. Working undercover with bad guys on their turf gave me an adrenaline rush.

Here is my story. The stories are true, and the events are real. The individuals involved are authentic; however, the names of certain persons have been changed to protect their privacy and for legal considerations.

I was born in Brooklyn, New York, and grew up in the neighborhood of Marine Park. Marine Park was a working-class neighborhood of residents of mostly Irish and Italian descent. I attended St. Thomas Aquinas Catholic Elementary School in Marine Park and attended St. Francis Preparatory School in Greenpoint, Brooklyn, where I played football.

Attending St. Francis Prep and playing football kept me on the right path for a law enforcement career. Attending St. Francis was one of the best decisions of my life. To get to the school, I traveled from Marine Park to Greenpoint, which was on the opposite end of Brooklyn. The trip took over an hour and required taking a city bus and three different subway lines. I actually had to take a subway line into Manhattan and take another line back into Brooklyn. That was how far Greenpoint was from Marine Park!

I traveled everyday with the Wall Street commuters, carrying my books and football equipment. I was fourteen years old and traveling far from home but never thought twice about it. Neither did my parents. That was just the way life was. Nothing worthwhile came easy. You had to work hard for success, and I was focused on academics and one day playing football in college.

Marine Park was a tough neighborhood, and there were many distractions, such as underage drinking, drugs, and fighting. With the competitive academic regimen of the Catholic school and a tough football practice, I didn't have time for the distractions. Marine Park was a neighborhood of police officers, firemen, and other civil servants. Being exposed to the police officers living on my block got me interested in a career as a police officer.

Upon graduation from high school, I attended Hobart College in Upstate New York where I continued to play football. Leaving Brooklyn to attend college was another great decision. Again, it got me away from the distractions of the neighborhood. Some of my friends were not so fortunate. Many did not attend college and went down the wrong path in life. Through my determination and a little luck, I did not go down that path.

In college, I began to think about a career in federal law enforcement with Secret Service or FBI. I was in college during two assassination attempts on President Ford's life. During this time, Secret Service received a lot of attention in the media, and I began to focus on a career with Secret Service.

I graduated from Hobart with a bachelor's degree in history, the first in my family to graduate from college. I applied to Secret Service and FBI, but because of lack of experience, I didn't have a chance at being hired. I began to take civil service tests for law enforcement positions to gain experience. One of the first positions offered to me was as a police officer with the Waterfront Commission of New York Harbor, and I readily accepted it.

The Waterfront Commission was established as a law enforcement and regulatory agency with jurisdiction in the port areas of New York and New Jersey. I was a sworn police officer in the State of New York and the State of New Jersey and conducted patrol and investigative duties.

It was not like a traditional police department with calls of service to residences for domestic or other issues, but we had plenty of activity with theft of cargo, truck hijackings, warehouse burglaries, industrial accidents, and traffic issues. I saw the influence of organized crime on the waterfront, and my dealings with tough port workers and the shady characters conducting business on the waterfront honed my investigative skills for my future position with Secret Service.

While employed as a police officer with the Waterfront Commission, I again applied to Secret Service. After an initial interview, written test, panel interview, and medical exam, I was offered a position as a special agent. I started my career on February 22, 1983, in the New York field office, which was located in the World Trade Center. I was sworn in by the special agent in charge, taken to the range to qualify with a Smith & Wesson Model 19 revolver, and assigned a government vehicle.

I received criminal investigative training at the Federal Law Enforcement Training Center in Georgia and specialized Secret Service training in Maryland and then hit the ground running. I spent the next six and a half years in New York, where I worked some of my best undercover assignments and criminal cases. My journey began.

THE GRIM REAPER

I slowly walked toward the back room of the social club, following the ominous figure in front of me. The Grim Reaper sat at a large oak desk, and I sat down across from him. In a thick Brooklyn accent, he said, "What can I do for you, kid?" My heart was pounding. I had just walked into the Wimpy Boys Social Club, a major organized crime meeting place.

I was not known by anyone in the club and could not believe that I was now sitting alone with the Grim Reaper. Knowing the reputation of this man, I was sure there were numerous other poor souls who made it to this exact spot, but never left the social club alive. I slowly began to speak, and as I uttered my first syllables, this ominous figure opened the top drawer of his desk and reached his hand inside.

My thoughts began to race. What was he doing? Was he getting a gun or just a pack of cigarettes? I instinctively placed my hand over the Smith & Wesson .38 revolver tucked in my waistband and told myself that no matter what would happen, I would leave that social club alive. Right now, I was vulnerable and sitting in the devil's den, and I had a quick decision to make.

In October 1985, at the US Secret Service New York field office, I was debriefing confidential source Sally Dogs with other members of the fraud squad and supervisor Ron Malone. Dogs was a street-smart Brooklyn kid who could walk the walk and talk the talk of the urban jungle. He was of Jewish descent, but came off as an Italian wannabe gangster and was kind of an annoying character.

He had this habit of flipping cigarettes in the air and catching them in his mouth, and everything he wore—from his Italian loafers to his Guess jean jacket—was purchased with counterfeit credit cards. Dogs called these fraudulent purchases mahooching, Brooklyn slang for getting over with phony plastic.

Dogs was just another guy in Brooklyn trying to survive, but now it was time to pay the piper. He was arrested for several credit card fraud schemes and was now trying to help himself out by providing information to Secret Service. Counterfeit credit cards and credit card fraud in New York and elsewhere were major problems in 1985, and Secret Service made it an investigative priority.

Counterfeiting credit cards was the bank robbery of the 1980s, and criminals were making hundreds of thousands of dollars with this illicit activity. This was the preferred crime because if caught, the penalty would be much less than sticking up a bank with a gun.

Dogs provided information that Gregory Scarpa Sr. was a major producer of counterfeit cards and that his crew was responsible for much of the credit card fraud in Brooklyn. He stated that through another individual, John Gena, we might be able to get inside the Scarpa organization.

Gregory Scarpa Sr., also known as the Grim Reaper, was a made member of the Colombo organized crime family. He and his crew conducted their criminal activities from the Wimpy Boys Social Club on Seventy-Sixth Street and Thirteenth Avenue in the Dyker Heights section of Brooklyn.

Scarpa had been involved in criminal activity for forty years, and by 1985, the fifty-eight-year-old gangster was at the peak of his power. He and his crew were involved in drug dealing, loan sharking, extortion, credit card fraud, and murder. If Secret Service could make a case against Scarpa, a very bad guy could be taken off the street.

A plan was set in motion to have an undercover agent meet with Gena to purchase counterfeit credit cards and, upon Gena's arrest, illicit his help as a confidential source against the Scarpa organization.

"I am assigning you as the undercover on this one," said Malone.

I was pleased to get the assignment and up for the challenge. Having been born and raised in Brooklyn, I was familiar with the ways of Brooklyn and had dealt with guys like Gena and Scarpa all my life. My years as a bouncer in the Brooklyn nightclub scene made me streetwise. I learned to deal with gangsters and street punks alike. I knew how they thought and how they reacted. I could talk like them, I could dress like them, and I could play the part of a Brooklyn wise guy.

I felt very confident in their environment, and I knew I could deal with them on their level. The supervisors in the New York office felt the same way. In the New York office, I was known as a street guy, someone who preferred criminal work over protective work.

I enjoyed working the street and dealing with Mafia criminals in Brooklyn. I preferred street work more than protecting and opening limousine doors for presidents and prime ministers at the Waldorf Astoria. Not that protection was a bad thing, but in Secret Service's world, I preferred to be on the street working criminal cases, and I especially enjoyed undercover work.

I walked into the second floor pool room at Kings Highway and Coney Island Avenue. The large room was filled with cigarette smoke and had the smell of stale beer. Sally Dogs made his rounds around the dimly lit room, fist-bumping the assortment of characters who were killing time and looking for their next score. Sally was very gregarious and seemed to know most of the two-bit gangsters in the room.

"Say hello to my man Tommy," exclaimed Sally as we came up to two guys at the end of the bar. "Where's Johnny Boy?" he asked, inquiring as to where John Gena might be.

"Ain't seen him today," said the taller guy on the left wearing a sharp leather jacket. "Usually comes in around four."

"Me and my man are looking to do some mahooching. We are hoping Johnny can hook us up."

"You will have to talk to him about that," said the guy on the right with the perfect haircut and diamond earring. He seemed very apprehensive and changed the subject, inquiring what the line was on the Jets game this Sunday.

Having grown up in the Marine Park section of Brooklyn, which was a short distance from the pool hall, I was hoping I wouldn't run into anyone I knew from the neighborhood. Growing up in Brooklyn was an asset for undercover work; however, it also had its negative side. If someone who knew me came into the pool room, it could jeopardize the undercover operation and possibly get me killed.

On a previous undercover operation, I was in a liquor store on Avenue P and McDonald Avenue, attempting to buy stolen US Treasury bonds from the owner. This location was a short distance from the home I grew up in and one block from my wife's family home.

As I was talking to the liquor store owner, the target of the investigation, I heard the door to the store open. As I glanced to my left, in walked Tommy Hines, a lifelong friend and a streetwise New York cop. I made eye contact with Tommy and gave him the look and quickly returned to my conversation with the liquor store owner. Tommy picked up on my vibe and didn't say a word to me. Being a good cop, Tommy realized what was going on and continued with his business.

Now in the pool hall, while waiting for Gena to show up, I scanned the faces of those around me and carefully watched who was coming and going. I thought about what had happened in the liquor store and hoped I would not see a familiar face in the crowd.

Dogs and I shot some pool, drank a couple of beers, and blended in with the crowd. We looked like two neighborhood guys hanging out with a lot of time to kill. Most of the guys in that pool hall were in the same boat. They were unemployed or on disability and had nothing productive to do.

They would come here every day, drink beer, shoot pool, and scheme for their next score. They had no money and no future and had delusions about getting rich through illegal activity. As I studied the crowd, I thought about what the future would hold for these guys.

I knew that if I came to this same pool hall in ten years, most of these guys would be sitting in the same bar stool. Some would be in jail, and some would be dead, killed by the same wise guys they aspired to be. Unfortunately, there were too many bars and pool halls throughout the borough of Brooklyn in neighborhoods such as Bay Ridge, Bensonhurst, Bath Beach, and Sheepshead Bay with hundreds of hopeless individuals in similar situations.

"Hey, what's shaking, Johnny?" exclaimed Dogs as Gena approached the bar. He gave Gena a hug and a kiss on the cheek, which was customary for wannabe wise guys. It was a show of respect they learned from watching too many mob movies. "Meet my man Tommy," said Dogs.

Gena gave me a look as if he was trying to size me up. "Hey, how ya doing?" I said in my Brooklyn accent, and I extended my hand. Gena hesitated and then shook my hand.

"Just trying to survive like everyone else," he said. "Where are you from, Tommy?"

"Sheepshead Bay over by Emmons Avenue," I said. I had an undercover New York State driver's license in the name of Tommy Ferraro with the address of 3030 Emmons Avenue in Sheepshead Bay. This was my cover story for undercover operations since 3030 Emmons Avenue was a large apartment building, and it would be very hard for bad guys to verify if I lived there or not.

Dogs chimed in. "Hey, Johnny, you gotta hook us up."

"With what?" said Gena.

"Shirts. We want to do some mahooching." *Shirts* was the term used by Brooklyn criminals for counterfeit credit cards. Unfortunately for them, law enforcement had known about that term early in the game.

Gena looked at Dogs, then looked at me and didn't say a word. He then said, "Hey, Dogs, why are you talking business? How well do you know this guy?"

"No problem, Johnny. Me and Tommy go way back. He is one of us."

"Ain't got any shirts," said Gena. "Can't get them. There is a problem."

"How about Greg?" asked Dogs.

Gena, in a very animated and pissed-off voice, said, "Fuck Greg. He's a nobody."

Gena was talking tough for my benefit, but he would never say that to Scarpa's face. If word got out about Gena's comment, he would be another of the Grim Reaper's victims, cut into pieces and dumped in a plastic garbage bag at the Staten Island landfill. In Scarpa's world, Gena was a nobody. If he could help Scarpa make money, fine; but if he became a problem, he was expendable.

"So what's the problem with the shirts?" asked Dogs.

"Don't want to talk now," said Gena.

He was apprehensive about talking in front of me, and he told Dogs he would see him in a few days. We played a couple of games of pool, had some beers, and parted ways with the understanding that Gena would reach out for Dogs in a couple of days.

"Where is the Rock?" said Pat Samson, the group leader of the New York office fraud squad.

"He's driving Dogs out to Long Island to pick up Gena," said Don Gilbert.

"He is doing what? Is he by himself? Get two units out there to pick him up. He shouldn't be out there alone," said Samson.

Rich "Rock" Enser was my partner in the fraud squad and to this day a lifelong friend, and now he was in an unsafe situation. On this same day, Gena contacted Dogs and set up another meeting at the pool hall. The plan was that I would go directly to the pool hall, and Rock would pick up Dogs at his residence and drive him there, thus ensuring that Dogs would show up.

Having Rock drive Dogs by himself was okay since Dogs was a vetted informant; however, driving sixty miles out to Long Island to pick up the target of the investigation was a problem. When Rock picked up Dogs, there was a change of plans.

Dogs said that Gena just contacted him and asked if he could drive him out to Long Island to pick him up. Being a good cop and being able to work undercover, Rock decided to act as a car service driver, taking Dogs out to Long Island.

Sometimes, in order to make a case, you have to make a quick decision, and Rock felt that the risk was minimal and made the decision to go. Luckily, the units from the New York office were able to pick up Rock's car on the Southern State Parkway and surveil him out to Long Island and, more importantly, back to Brooklyn with Gena in the vehicle.

I was sitting at the bar when Dogs and Gena walked in.

"Took you long enough. Where have you been?"

"Detour to Long Island, but we made it," said Dogs.

"Okay, let's get right to the point. I have been waiting here a long time." I turned my attention to Gena. "Johnny, are you going to be able to help us out with those shirts we talked about?"

"We got a problem. Nobody has got any shirts," said Gena.

"What is the problem?" I asked.

"The shirts need holy grams," he exclaimed.

I gave him a puzzled look and said, "Holy grams? What the hell are you talking about?"

"You know. Holy grams, those stickers that are put on the new shirts. The banks put them on now. Tough to use the shirt without them."

I finally realized what Gena was talking about. Around this time, Mastercard and Visa, as an anti-counterfeiting measure, began placing holograms on credit cards. They were silver stickers with a logo that changed dimensions when held at different angles and was virtually impossible to counterfeit. According to Gena, this new feature was taking a toll on the bad guys.

Dogs, Gena, and I played a couple of games of pool and shot the breeze for a while, then parted ways. I made several other attempts to contact Gena about the shirts, but nothing ever worked out. The case was at an impasse, and we needed to find a new way to get to the Scarpa organization.

It was decided that I was going to walk into Wimpy Boys cold, sell myself as a wise guy, and make the case. This was a very ambitious plan when dealing with Brooklyn mobsters, but we had no alternative at this point. I was going to walk in with Dogs, who claimed he knew some guys who hung out there, and I was going to meet face-to-face with the Grim Reaper.

"Never going to happen," said a veteran NYPD detective assigned to the Brooklyn District Attorney's Office. "We have been trying to get this guy for years. He is too cautious. He will not meet with anyone he does not know." However, the die was cast. I was going to stroll into the Wimpy Boys, and I was going to meet with a stone-cold killer. It was a long shot, but we were determined to give it a try.

The information that Gena passed to me about the holograms on credit cards was true. We learned that Scarpa's credit card fraud activities were limited because of these new anti-counterfeiting measures, and my cover story was developed. I was going to pose as a guy who worked at the plant where these cards were manufactured and who could provide them to Scarpa.

This was going to be a sting operation wherein I would provide the illegal product to the target. This was a commonly used technique in law enforcement investigations and was not considered entrapment under federal law. Through our contacts in the credit card industry, Secret Service was able to obtain a couple of blank Visas and Mastercards with holograms for use in the investigation.

The idea was to show Scarpa one of these cards to get his interest and set the hook. On October 29, 1985, the plan was set into motion, and a briefing was conducted at the New York field office prior to the start of the undercover operation.

"Tommy, you need to wear a wire for this meeting," exclaimed Malone. A wire was a transmitter that I would be wearing on my body that allowed covering teams to hear what was going on. "For your safety, the surveillance teams need to know what's going on inside."

Malone had a point. I would be dealing with a dangerous individual, so wearing a wire made sense; however, I felt differently.

"If this guy is as cautious as they say he is, wearing a wire is not a good idea. If the wire is somehow discovered, it could put me in a very bad position," I explained to Malone. "I feel more comfortable meeting him for the first time without the wire."

Malone insisted on the wire, but I was adamant that for this first meeting, I would not wear one. I felt that if there was a problem, I would be able to get myself out of the social club. I felt that wearing a wire for the first meeting had more downside than upside, and Malone finally agreed. As we will see later, it was a good thing he did.

The plan was to have several two-agent teams in the area of the club who could observe me enter and leave. Once inside, if I could not meet Scarpa, I was to leave immediately. If I did meet with him, I was to limit my time inside to half an hour. Any more time than that would signal trouble, and the covering teams would come in.

So it was all set. That afternoon, I was going to enter the Wimpy Boys Social Club and try to meet with a very dangerous member of the Brooklyn Mafia. I wore my Guess jean jacket, gray leather loafers, diamond pinky ring, and large gold bracelet. I looked like a Brooklyn wise guy. I was ready for action and felt very comfortable in my role.

My heart was pounding as we entered the door of the social club. Suddenly, all eyes were upon us. The room was filled with cigarette smoke, several guys were playing cards at a small table with a bottle of Johnnie Walker Black nearby, and Frank Sinatra's "Summer Wind" was playing on the jukebox.

"Hey, this is a private club," someone shouted from the back of the room.

"Just looking for Johnny Gena," explained Dogs.

Several guys in the club gave the impression that they knew Dogs, which eased the tension somewhat. Again, someone shouted from the rear of the room, "He is not here. Haven't seen him for a while."

"How about Greg? Is he around?" asked Sally Dogs. "We may have some business for him."

Suddenly, we were approached by an individual from the back of the room. I recognized him as Greg Scarpa Jr., son of the Grim Reaper. "Who is asking?" said Scarpa Jr.

"Sally Dogs, a friend of Johnny Gena. My man Tommy had some shirt business for him, but since he ain't around, maybe Greg is interested."

Scarpa Jr. was a street thug who ran a drug-dealing operation in Brooklyn and Staten Island and was as vicious as his father. He gave me a cold stare, looked me up and down, and said, "Wait here." I couldn't believe we had gotten this far.

The Grim Reaper walked toward us from the back room of the social club. He was in his middle to late fifties and stocky with the look of an ex-boxer. He had bags under his eyes and a worn look about him. It looked like thirty years of criminal activity and the partying that went with it was catching up with him.

Despite his worn look, I still knew he was a very dangerous figure who would kill me at the drop of a hat. I knew I had to keep up my guard and be ready to react should the situation warrant it. Scarpa gave us an icy stare and looked both of us over.

"What's up?" he asked his son.

The son looked at me and said, "He's got some shirt business with Johnny Gena, but Johnny has not been around."

"Oh, shirt business," exclaimed Scarpa while looking me over, trying to size me up. Scarpa pointed to me and said, "Take a walk back to my office." I told Dogs to wait for me up front, and I followed Scarpa back to his office, and we sat at his large desk. As I previously noted, Scarpa immediately opened the desk drawer and put his hand inside.

As quickly as Scarpa had put his hand in the desk drawer, he removed it and closed the drawer, and my apprehension began to subside. No gun, no cigarettes, nothing! I eased my hand from the .38 revolver in my waistband and looked Scarpa in the eye.

"Hey, kid. What can I do for you?" said Scarpa for a second time. My focus was now off his hand movement and the drawer, and I focused on his words.

"I was working on a deal with Johnny Gena, but I can't get in touch with him."

"A deal? Where are you from, kid?" Scarpa said quizzically.

"Sheepshead Bay over by Emmons Avenue," I replied.

"Why did you come see me about this deal?" asked Scarpa.

"I know Johnny from the pool hall over on Coney Island Avenue. He mentioned that he hung out at this club and he had done some business with you," I said.

"Johnny talks too much," Scarpa said angrily. "I don't know you. Why would I do a deal with you?" Scarpa growled. "I give you credit, though. You've got a lot of balls walking in here."

"Talk to Johnny," I said. "He knows what I can do."

"So what can you do?" Scarpa snapped back.

"This is what I can do."

I reached into my shirt pocket and pulled out one of the credit cards we received from our contacts in the industry and placed it on the desk in front of Scarpa. The card had no number, but it had the issuing bank name, the Mastercard logo, the magnetic stripe on the back, and the all-important hologram.

Scarpa's eyes opened wide when he saw what was in front of him. "Very interesting. Where did you get this?" he asked.

"I work at the plant where these are made, and I can get more."

"You can? How many?" he asked.

I knew I had him hooked. He seemed to have dropped all reservations about not knowing me and was now focusing on the card in his hand and the amount of money he could make.

"For now, I can get you three hundred more," I said, "A hundred fifty Mastercards and a hundred fifty Visas."

"And what do you want?" Scarpa asked.

"How about thirty dollars apiece, nine grand for all of them?"

I could tell Scarpa's wheels were turning and the hook was set. Once those cards were embossed with stolen legitimate credit card numbers and those numbers were encoded on the cards' magnetic stripe, they had a potential value of $5,000 each or 1.5 million dollars! Scarpa's crew had the sources to steal the numbers and the technical knowledge to emboss and encode the cards, so for a small investment of money and time, his score would be very profitable.

Scarpa, totally unguarded, said, "How about you give me a call next week and we can have another meeting here? If you are ready to do business, maybe we can do the deal."

Within the agreed upon half hour of entering the club, I left, hopped in the undercover vehicle with Dogs, and drove away from Wimpy Boys. My tension eased as the realization of what I had just done set in. I could not believe that, against all odds, I had just met with one of New York's most notorious Mafia leaders. I was able to convince him I was a criminal and was on the verge of possibly taking down his criminal enterprise.

As I pulled away from the club, in my rearview mirror, I observed my covering teams following me. This was done as a precaution to ensure I was not followed. I turned on my radio that was hidden in the glove box of the vehicle, and as I approached Thirty-Ninth Street on the Brooklyn-Queens Expressway, I was given the all-clear signal.

Not being followed was a good sign that I had done my job well and that I could now head back to Secret Service's office at Six World Trade Center. At the office, I debriefed the squad as to what had happened. The guys could not believe what had just happened. According to Brooklyn District Attorney's Office detectives, I was the first undercover law enforcement officer to meet directly with Greg Scarpa Sr. The case was looking very promising.

On November 5, 1985, I went to the undercover telephone line that was installed in the New York field office and dialed the Wimpy Boys Social Club. The phone was answered in a very recognizable Brooklyn accent.

"I'm looking for Big Greg." The term *Big* was a Brooklyn way of distinguishing between father and son and mother and daughter.

"Who are you?" the voice asked apprehensively.

"Tommy. I met with Greg last week, and he said to give him a call today."

"Hang on," the voice said, now less guarded.

The Grim Reaper got on the line. "Hey, kid. How are you doing?"

"Doing good," I said. "Calling you back like you asked me to."

"How did you make out?" asked Scarpa.

"All set on my end," I replied.

"Good. Let's not talk too much on the phone. Come to the club tomorrow at about two o'clock, and we can take care of what we spoke about."

"That sounds good. See you tomorrow." Little did the Grim Reaper know that the telephone line was recorded and that Secret Service was slowly building a case to put him out of business.

The week prior to my phone call to Scarpa, Secret Service was able to obtain the three hundred blank Visas and Mastercards with holograms from our contacts in the credit card industry. Scarpa was very well-known to them for his fraudulent credit card activities, and they were more than glad to help bring him down.

The following morning, a squad briefing was held to discuss my undercover meeting later that afternoon. As always, the primary focus of the meeting was the safety of the undercover. Second was the protection of the three hundred credit cards. It would not look good for Secret Service or our partners in the credit card industry if we somehow lost these cards.

The deal was going to be a buy bust. A buy bust was a deal wherein when the money and credit cards exchanged hands, the covering teams would move in and arrest the suspect.

"Tommy, are you wearing a wire on this one?" Malone asked.

"I don't know, Ron. Let me think about it."

"Probably should," he said, "but it's up to you."

For my safety, for the protection of the credit cards, and to have recorded evidence for the prosecution of the case, I decided to wear a wire. I felt that since I had met Scarpa once already and got a good feeling that he did not suspect anything, wearing a wire would be less risky for this meeting.

I would be wearing a KEL transmitter, which would permit the agents covering me to hear what was going on through their car radios or handheld radios. I would also permit all conversations to be recorded should they be needed for judicial proceedings.

Wearing a wire made sense at this point; however, as we will see later, it almost was a disastrous decision for my safety and the success of the operation. It was also decided to cut out Sally Dogs at this point. Since I had developed a relationship with the Grim Reaper, I would meet him without Dogs.

"Tommy, you are not to trip with this guy," said Malone during the briefing. *Tripping* was a term used when an undercover agent left the agreed-upon meeting location with the target. Tripping put the safety of the undercover and credit cards at risk should the undercover be lost by the covering teams.

"I know. I won't trip," I said.

The plan was that I would meet Scarpa at Wimpy Boys, but leave the credit cards in a vehicle outside. This would help prevent a robbery and leave me less exposed. Once I met him inside and knew he had the cash, I would get him outside to complete the deal at the car. This was a tough order for a cautious mafioso like Scarpa, but the safest way to do the deal.

Once the deal was concluded, the covering teams listening on the wire transmitter would converge on the vehicle, arrest Scarpa, and recover the credit cards. The covering teams would immediately execute a search and seizure warrant on the Wimpy Boys Social Club. The warrant would give them the opportunity to search the club for any additional contraband or intelligence information.

It was decided that I would drive to the club with a second agent or bag man in an undercover Cadillac. That agent would wait right outside the club with the credit cards sitting on the front seat. The agent assigned, Jimmy Venzo, was a streetwise former New Jersey State Police and a good choice for the assignment. As always during my undercover assignments, I had my five-shot revolver tucked in my waistband just in case things didn't go as planned.

"Jimmy, as I told Tommy, no tripping. Keep the car outside the club, and don't move it until Tommy comes out. Do not go anywhere else to do the deal," exclaimed Malone.

"Got it, Ron, no tripping," replied Jimmy.

On November 6, 1985, the undercover Cadillac pulled up outside the social club. I could feel my heart starting to beat faster. Working undercover gave me an adrenaline rush, and I was both excited and apprehensive. I wanted this deal to go right, and I wanted to stay alive.

As I entered the social club, all eyes were upon me again. The room was filled with cigar smoke, and I noticed a guy at the end of the bar smoking a big stogie and downing a shot of scotch.

"Looking for Big Greg," I said.

"Who are you?" asked the guy with the stogie very cautiously.

"Tell Greg Tommy is here. He is expecting me."

Just as I finished my sentence, I saw a hulking figure walking toward me through the smoke. It was the Grim Reaper.

"How are you doing, Tommy?"

"Doing well, but I'd be better if I had one of those cigars," I replied.

"Stay away from them. They will kill you," Scarpa sarcastically replied. Scarpa looked at me and motioned to go outside. "Don't want to do business in the club. Let's go outside," he said.

I couldn't believe it. I was going to try to get him outside the club, and he was taking care of this problem for me. I thought, *This is too easy*, and I was right. When we got outside, Scarpa pointed to a Buick Riviera parked in front. The Riviera was a typical wise-guy car of that time.

"Let's take a ride around the corner. I don't want to do business in front of the club," Scarpa said cautiously.

I started to process what was happening. Was I going to get in that car and maybe not get out alive? Did he have three of his crew waiting around the corner to rip me off? Why did he leave the safety of his club to meet me outside?

As these thoughts raced through my brain, I made a quick decision to get in his car. I felt that with Jimmy covering me closely and the covering teams listening to everything on the transmitter, I would be all right. However, I would be breaking the cardinal rule of undercover work: don't trip with the target.

"Greg, we are just going around the corner, right?" I asked.

"Yeah. We will make a right on Seventy-Sixth Street and go down the block a little way," he replied.

I pointed to the Cadillac behind his vehicle and said, "My guy has the shirts in the car."

"Have him follow us down the block," he said.

I couldn't believe it, Scarpa was breaking all the rules of how wise guys worked. He left the safety of his club to do a deal with someone he met only one time before who had a second guy with him he did not know. Either I did one hell of a convincing undercover job, or we were going to get ripped off around the corner.

I felt good about the deal and thought it was the former. I motioned to Jimmy to follow us and got in Scarpa's vehicle. Jimmy, being a good street cop, picked up on my vibe and began to follow me. As I later learned, all hell broke loose at the field office when I got into Scarpa's car. Malone was on the radio, wondering what the hell I was doing and imploring the covering agents not to lose me.

As the Grim Reaper said, we made a right on Seventy-Sixth Street with Jimmy right behind me. We pulled over to the side of the street, and Scarpa pulled out an envelope with $9,000 in hundred-dollar bills. My eyes lit up when I saw the cash, and I knew it was not a rip-off. We had him!

I exited Scarpa's vehicle and went back to the Cadillac and gave Jimmy a big grin. He also knew we had him. I returned to Scarpa's vehicle with the credit cards, handed them to him, and took the cash. I told Scarpa, "With this cash, I'm going to take a trip to Acapulco." The prearranged signal to the covering agents to move in was the word *Acapulco*.

For what seemed an eternity, I sat there with Scarpa, waiting for the troops to arrive. Suddenly, a car came to a screeching halt next to the Riviera, and out jumped Pat Samson. He pulled Scarpa's door open and dragged him out of the car.

I remember Samson shoving his badge in Scarpa's face and asking, "What does this say?"

Scarpa meekly replied, "US Secret Service."

"Yes, it's the US Secret Service, and you're under arrest," Samson replied.

Scarpa had a stunned look on his face, and for the first time in many years, he was under arrest. He was placed in handcuffs and transported in Samson's vehicle. To keep my undercover role intact, I was also handcuffed and placed in a second vehicle. Responding agents also secured the credit cards and cash.

We both were transported back to the Wimpy Boys Social Club. Upon arrival, I observed the rest of the covering teams executing the search warrant. Traffic was blocked by Secret Service vehicles, and onlookers were beginning to gather across the street.

I saw my buddy Rock Enser holding six club members at bay with a shotgun outside the club. All had their hands high in the air, and all were wearing the polyester jogging suits that were typical for portly wannabe gangsters in the 1980s.

One of the guys' pants started to fall as he held his hands high, but with a shotgun trained on him, he dared not bring his hands down to pull up his pants. I heard him ask Rock if he could pull up his pants for him. Rock looked at him and said, "Pull your own damn pants up. I'm not pulling them up."

With that, the guy dropped his hands and pulled up his pants. This was a comical moment that helped ease the intensity of the situation I was just in. I was still in handcuffs, standing by a car in front of the club, when I started thinking about everything that occurred over the past two weeks.

One thing that stood out in my mind was my first meeting with Scarpa when he placed his hand inside his desk drawer. I was still wondering what he was looking for. It could have been innocuous, but something told me there was more to it.

I spoke to one of the agents conducting the search, explained the situation of my first meeting, and asked them to search the desk drawer. A few minutes later, he came back and told me what was found. There was no gun, no knife; however, an interesting device was found. Located in the top desk drawer was an electronic device. It was described as about six inches long with a wire antenna and red LED light. Interesting, but what was it?

I was transported back to the New York field office, and as soon as we cleared the area, my handcuffs were removed. I felt good since I was in them for over an hour and they had begun to cut off some circulation. Upon arrival, I saw Malone. He was a little upset that I had left the club with Scarpa; however, the deal went well, and that would be the last I would hear of it.

I immediately went to the interview room adjacent to where Scarpa was being interviewed and observed what was going on. Scarpa appeared to be in disbelief of what had just happened. He was not saying much at that point as was typical of Brooklyn wise guys of the day. Just then, the enormity of what we had accomplished set in. We had arrested one of the most notorious Mafia leaders in New York, and now he was facing a lengthy jail sentence.

Scarpa was one of the highest-profile mafia leaders ever arrested by Secret Service. If all went well, we would be taking a very dangerous criminal off the street for ten years, which was the amount of time Scarpa was facing in this case. I knew how dangerous he was and began to think of how that had an impact on me.

Should he make bail, he or members of his crew would be looking for Tommy Ferraro. Since I lived in Brooklyn and not too far from the Wimpy Boys Social Club, I felt that this could be a problem for me and my fiancé. Additionally, my mother and father and my future mother-in-law and father-in-law lived in Brooklyn. God forbid I run into Scarpa with my family members present while out at a restaurant or shopping.

I began to wonder how long I would have to keep my undercover role going. I approached the supervisors in the field office about my concerns, and it was decided that I would let Scarpa know exactly who I was. Once he knew I was a federal agent, the risks of an encounter with him or a member of his crew on the streets of Brooklyn would be minimized. However, I would never trust him or anyone in his circle, and I would always have an off-duty weapon with me when out and about.

I walked into the interview room where Scarpa was handcuffed to a large desk. His eyes opened wide, and he gave me a puzzled look. I could tell he was wondering what was going on. He saw me get arrested, but now I was walking in on him unescorted and not in handcuffs. I threw my Secret Service badge and commission book on the desk in front of him and told him, "Take a look."

He picked up the identification and began to shake his head. "You were good, kid. That's all I'm going to say."

"You don't have to say anything. I just want to let you know who I am and where I stand. I don't want any misunderstanding about this."

"I got you, kid. There will be no misunderstanding," he replied.

A few days later, we received a report from Secret Service Headquarters concerning the electronic device that was seized in Scarpa's desk. It was determined that the device was used to detect transmitters. If someone came into proximity of the device with a transmitter, the red LED light would light up.

I looked at the report and could not believe what I was reading and realized how lucky I was. At my first meeting with Scarpa, had I worn a transmitter, at best, I would have been thrown out of the club; at worst, I could have been killed.

During my second meeting, had Scarpa not come out of his office and motioned me to go outside, the plan was for me to meet him in the office wearing the transmitter. Who knew how that would have ended? My instincts were good not to wear a wire to the first meeting; however, we got very lucky at the second meeting!

On the evening of Scarpa's arrest, the chief of Organized Crime Strike Force for the Eastern District of New York showed up at the New York field office to interview him. For such a high-ranking member of the US Attorney's Office to come to the field office at that time of night made me realize what a big deal the arrest of Scarpa was.

The chief offered Scarpa a place in the government's Witness Protection Program if he would cooperate and become a Mafia informant. Scarpa politely declined the offer. The chief informed Scarpa that he would be the US attorney prosecuting the case and that they would talk more at a later date.

Scarpa was fingerprinted, photographed, and processed at the field office and then lodged at the Metropolitan Correctional Center in Lower Manhattan pending a bail hearing. Several days later, Scarpa appeared before a federal magistrate and was released on a $300,000 bail. Scarpa was facing a ten-year jail sentence and a $250,000 fine.

At a subsequent meeting with the chief of the Strike Force, Scarpa made a bombshell revelation. Scarpa revealed that he was a confidential informant for the FBI. This revelation caused the FBI to be on the defensive, and rightly so.

It was later learned through Freedom of Information Act (FOIA) requests that Scarpa had been providing information to the FBI since the early 1960s, and a memo from the FBI director as recent as March 15, 1985, authorized a $15,000 payment to Scarpa. I began to wonder how a bad guy like Scarpa could operate his criminal enterprise undetected by the FBI, an agency he had been providing information to for thirty years!

Despite the arrest, an FOIA-obtained FBI memo indicated that Scarpa was retained as a confidential informant, and the FBI went to great lengths to protect him from the Secret Service credit card arrest. Despite the FBI's attempts to protect Scarpa, the chief of the Organized Crime Strike Force pressed the case, and Scarpa w indicted on a four-count indictment in the Eastern District of New York. However, through the intervention of the FBI and, in particular, Scarpa's handling agent in the New York office as revealed in FOIA-requested FBI memos, it appeared that Scarpa got off lightly.

On June 18, 1986, Scarpa pled guilty to one count of the indictment and was sentenced to five years of probation instead of the ten years of incarceration he was facing. Scarpa's criminal activity continued after his guilty plea on the credit card charges. He was intricately involved in the Colombo family wars of the 1990s, during which more than a dozen people lost their lives, all while he continued to provide information to the FBI.

I often wonder how many of those lives could have been saved had the FBI not intervened in the credit card case. It is noted that Scarpa's FBI handling agent was indicted in 2006 by the Brooklyn District Attorney's Office for his alleged complicity in numerous crimes that Scarpa committed while he was responsible for directing Scarpa; however, the charges were dismissed at trial. I will let the reader decide for themselves whether the FBI turned a blind eye to Scarpa's criminal activity while he was providing information to them.

WISE GUYS FROM CANAL STREET

"**A**ny Manhattan check agent, pick up line one" was the call over the intercom in the New York field office in late 1983. In the 1980s, most federal payments for pensions, social security benefits, and welfare benefits were paid using a paper check. There was very limited electronic deposit like we have today. These checks were often stolen in the mail and cashed fraudulently.

During this time, the New York field office had a check forgery squad investigating stolen and forged US Treasury checks. Being a newly assigned check forgery agent, I picked up the line and started talking to an individual who would later become my first confidential informant. The individual was looking for Rich Schena, a former agent of the New York office who was recently transferred. I told him that Schena was no longer in the office and asked if I could help him.

"You will not believe what's going on over on Canal Street," he said.

"Oh yeah? What's going on?" I asked.

He began to tell me a story of this mob guy Sam and another individual named Bernie who operated two jewelry shops on Canal Street. He claimed that they were fencing stolen property through their shops and that in particular, they were purchasing stolen US Treasury checks.

I asked him how he knew that, and he stated that he was a former employee in one of the shops. I asked him his name, and he replied, "Nick D'Agostino." I was very interested in the Treasury check aspect of the information, and I made arrangements to meet with him at the office later that afternoon.

Nick was a streetwise Hispanic kid in his early twenties from the Bushwick section of Brooklyn. His real name was Hector Santiago, but he used the Italian Nick D'Agostino when conducting business on the street. Before his arrival, I contacted SA Schena, who advised that Nick had provided him information in the past and that his information was reliable.

Later that day, Nick arrived at the New York field office and told me a very detailed story about the criminal activity being conducted at the jewelry shops. He told the story of Sam Agro and Bernie Golomb, the operators of the jewelry shops at 201 and 203 Canal Street in the Chinatown section of Manhattan.

He stated that Sam was a guy with Mafia ties and that Bernie was a Russian immigrant. He claimed that they ran a major fencing operation and that they purchased stolen items from individuals from all over the city. He stated that they had been conducting their criminal activity with impunity for several years and that he personally witnessed this criminal activity while an employee of one of the shops. He stated that he was no longer an employee and that he wanted to help law enforcement put an end to the criminal activity.

I asked him what his motivation was, and he stated that he worked with Secret Service in the past and that they treated him fairly and paid him well. He stated that he was currently unemployed and needed the money. He stated that he would be willing to introduce someone to Sam and Bernie.

I began to conduct my background research on Sam and Bernie and prepared for the possible introduction of an undercover agent at the jewelry shop. Through information provided by the Waterfront Commission of New York Harbor, I identified Sam as Salvatore Agro, a made member of the Magaddino crime family of Buffalo, New York. Through immigration sources, I was able to identify Bernie as Benzion Golomb, an immigrant from Uzbekistan in the Soviet Union. Both had prior criminal records.

Management at the field office approved an undercover operation, and I was assigned as the undercover agent. The plan was to have Nick introduce me to Sam and Bernie, gain their confidence, and ultimately sell them stolen property in a reverse sting operation. The stolen property would be in the form of spurious US Treasury checks that were printed by the Department of the Treasury for investigations of this nature. This was my first undercover assignment as a Secret Service agent.

The following day, I met with Nick at the field office. I told him the game plan and had him make a recorded phone call to Sam or Bernie. Nick spoke to an employee; however, he was unable to speak to Sam or Bernie. It was decided that I would walk into the shop with Nick and try to meet them directly.

Later that week, Nick and I went to 201 Canal Street in an attempt to meet with Sam or Bernie. We were covered by two agents who had a visual on the location from a vehicle on Canal Street. We got lucky. When we walked in, Sam was behind the counter. He looked like a tough guy and definitely fit the profile for a mob guy. He was in his late fifties with graying hair and a muscular build. He had the look of an ex-boxer or mob enforcer.

Nick introduced me as Tommy, a friend from Brooklyn. Nick explained that we had some business to take care of. Upon hearing that we wanted to conduct business, Sam became very guarded. His reaction was typical for a mob guy since he didn't know me.

He stated that any business we had to take care of should be done with Bernie. We spent some time talking to Sam but did not talk business or any criminal activity. I wanted to make Sam feel comfortable with me so next time, he might not be so guarded. We left the shop with the understanding that we would contact Bernie.

Later that day, Nick was able to contact Bernie by telephone. The conversation was recorded. Nick spoke openly during the conversation, and Bernie was less guarded than his partner. He explained that his friend Tommy had some paper he wanted to sell and that the paper was federal. *Paper* was cryptic for checks, and *federal* was cryptic for Treasury.

Bernie seemed very interested and sounded like he had complete trust in Nick. He advised Nick to give him a call and set up a time to drop off the paper. Nick advised that he would call later in the week and set up a time. Several days later, the spurious checks we ordered from the Department of the Treasury arrived at the field office, and we were ready to make the deal.

Nick made several attempts to contact Bernie by telephone and finally reached him. Again, we recorded the call. He advised that we were ready to drop off the paper. We had five spurious Treasury checks totaling about $7,000 and he told Bernie that we had five pieces of paper and that we needed 30 percent. He never spoke actual dollar amounts since you wouldn't talk like that on the phone.

Bernie agreed to the 30 percent and said to drop off the paper at the store on Canal Street. He said that he would be out of town for a few days and to leave the paper with Sam. He said that he would settle up with us when he returned. That scenario worked perfectly for us. We already had Bernie implicated by his conversation on the phone. With Sam receiving the checks, he also would be part of the illegal scheme.

The following day, Nick and I went to the jewelry store at 201 Canal Street to drop of the paper. Sam was behind the counter, and Nick told him we had something to drop off for Bernie. I reached into my jacket pocket and removed the spurious Treasury checks, which were in a white envelope. Sam looked at me, hesitated for a moment, and said, "I will take it, but I don't want to know what's in it."

With that statement, Sam took the envelope and placed it behind the counter. Now we had him also! I was very surprised that a made guy was this naive. I wondered if he really thought that saying that he didn't want to know what was in it would protect him from the law. Well, in any case, he was now part of the conspiracy. We still needed to get a face-to-face meeting between me and Bernie, and we began to work on that.

Several days later, Nick made a recorded call to the shop looking for Bernie and was able to connect with him. Bernie acknowledged that he received the paper and that all went well with it. He stated that he had our 30 percent, and we made arrangements to meet at the jewelry shop to get it.

Later that afternoon, Nick and I met Bernie at the shop. I could tell that Bernie felt very comfortable with me, and he readily handed me an envelope with $2,100, which was our end of the transaction. He began to talk freely about the deal and said that he would take as many Treasury checks as we could provide as they were very easy to negotiate.

I told him I was working on getting another batch and that I would reach out to him once I had them. We ordered another batch of checks from the Department of the Treasury, and when they arrived, I contacted Bernie directly. Since Bernie was comfortable with me, it was decided to cut out Nick and deal directly with Bernie myself.

I placed a recorded call to the shop and told him I had some more paper a little more valuable than the last batch and that, again, I needed 30 percent. Bernie stated that it would not be a problem, and we set up a meeting for the next day at the Wong Kee restaurant in 103 Mott Street in the Chinatown section of Manhattan.

The following day, a surveillance van was set up directly in front of the restaurant. The two agents inside had cameras to photograph the meeting and a receiver to monitor and record my conversations with Bernie. Since my previous interaction with Bernie went well, I felt comfortable wearing a wire to the meeting.

I arrived at the restaurant first and got a table by the front window, facing the door. This table gave the agents in the surveillance van a perfect view of the meeting. When Bernie walked in the door, I motioned him over to the table. After some small talk about what a great restaurant the Wong Kee was, we got down to business.

Bernie spoke openly and seemed very comfortable during the meeting. I told him that I had eight pieces of paper just like the last batch totaling $10,000. I handed Bernie the envelope with the eight spurious US Treasury checks, and he placed it in his jacket pocket. He then removed a wad of bills from his pants pocket and began to count it under the table, out of the view of the restaurant patrons.

Once counted, he folded the bills and discretely handed me $3,000 in hundred-dollar bills. Our food arrived a short time later, and we enjoyed a great Chinese lunch. After eating, I excused myself and went to a downstairs restroom while Bernie stayed at the table. Once in the bathroom, I locked the door, removed a walkie-talkie that was hidden under my shirt, and quietly advised the agents in the van that the deal was complete and that Bernie had the checks.

The agents in the van acknowledged and set in place the next stage of the operation. The plan was that if Bernie completed the deal, he would be arrested at the restaurant. Two agents had already pulled up outside the restaurant when I said goodbye and left Bernie at the table.

The agents entered, identified themselves, and placed a shocked Bernie under arrest. Simultaneously, agents went to 201 Canal Street and arrested Sam Agro on an arrest warrant for his part in the first transaction. Both were transported to the New York field office in the World Trade Center for processing and interview.

I interviewed Salvatore "Sam" Agro first. Agro was an old-school wise guy and a made member of the Magaddino crime family of Buffalo, New York, conducting his business in New York City. I identified myself as a federal agent, and I could tell he was very surprised by that revelation. However, he was a stand-up guy, and in a matter-of-fact way, he told me, "I don't care what the fuck you do to me. I ain't saying anything. Do what you gotta do."

That was my first encounter with a true mob guy who stuck to the Mafia code of Omertà, the code of silence. He was a dying breed as the 1980s saw numerous high-level mobsters break the code of silence to cut a better deal for themselves. Agro was not that type of guy. He would not say a word and took whatever punishment was coming his way.

When the arrests hit the New York newspapers, we began to get a flood of information about Bernie and Sam. The case was a simple buy-bust case that was about to get very complicated. A couple of days after the newspaper articles, Rock Enser picked up a phone call from NYPD detective Joe Guarduno from the Staten Island Crimes Against Property Squad.

"Hey, how you doing?" Guarduno said. "I hear you guys are working a case on a couple of wise guys from Canal Street," he continued in a thick New York accent. Guarduno told Enser about a case he was working regarding checks that were stolen from the Mariner Family Home, a home for retired merchant seamen on Staten Island.

I later spoke to Guarduno, who advised me that his case pointed to 201 Canal Street as the location where the stolen checks were fenced. He advised that the checks were then fraudulently negotiated for a loss of $80,000 to the Mariner Family Home.

I began to work a joint investigation with the NYPD on this aspect of the case. Additionally, we began to receive information from local police departments in New York and New Jersey regarding arrested burglars in their jurisdiction who pointed to Bernie and Sam and 201 Canal Street as the individuals who fenced the stolen items. We now began working with local authorities on the stolen property cases.

We interviewed numerous burglars who provided information and agreed to testify against Sam and Bernie. We identified the individual who stole the checks from the Mariner Family Home, who, in turn, identified Sam and Bernie as the individuals who fenced the checks.

We completed a forensic analysis of the checks and identified fingerprints of both Sam and Bernie on the checks. We had a solid case. We had a hand-to-hand exchange between me and Bernie, and we had Sam accepting a package directly from me on behalf of Bernie. Additionally, we had numerous individuals who pointed to both Sam and Bernie as the fences for stolen property and forensic evidence connecting both of them to the stolen Mariner Family Home checks.

Numerous suspects and both Sam and Bernie were indicted in the Southern District of New York on a multicount indictment for the purchase of stolen US Treasury checks, receipt of stolen property, credit card fraud, and the fraudulent receipt and negotiation of the Mariner Family Home checks.

Sam, being the stand-up, old-school mobster, pled guilty to the indictment and in July 1984 was sentenced to a ten-year jail sentence in the Southern District of New York. Agro was released from federal custody on July 29, 1988, after completing four years of his sentence.

Bernie was another story. He decided to go to trial with a compelling case against him and was convicted of all counts against him. During the trial, a question arose regarding the credit card fraud charge. In evidence was a photo of Bernie allegedly sitting in a hotel on the island of Jamaica where numerous fraudulent credit card transactions were made. Of course, he denied that he was ever at that hotel.

To resolve the issue, the judge directed that someone travel to Jamaica, locate the particular hotel, and take a picture of the exact spot where Bernie was sitting in the photo. The judge would then let that individual testify to what they would find, a daunting task, to say the least. We were in the middle of the trial, and it would be very difficult to travel to Jamaica quickly and get back with the information the judge requested before the trial was over.

You guessed it. I was given the assignment to fly to Jamaica! My supervisor at the time had about fifteen years on the job, and when he found out about my assignment, he tried to help. He said that he had contacts within the Jamaican police and that he would arrange for them to help with my assignment. He told me that once I flew into Montego Bay, I should go to the local police station, and everything would be set up for their assistance.

I arrived in Montego Bay and went directly to the police station. I identified myself to the officers at the front desk and advised that the commanding officer was expecting me. The commanding officer was contacted and came to the front desk. He gave me a puzzled look and said he didn't know what I was talking about. I guess my boss's contacts were not as good as he thought!

At this time, I had only about a year on the job, but I knew I was not going to get any help from the local police. I decided to get the job done on my own. The hotel I was looking for was in Ocho Rios, about seventy miles from Montego Bay. I rented a car, got a map of Jamaica, and headed off to Ocho Rios.

It was definitely an experience. I drove on the left side of the road English style for the first time, and I encountered several police roadblocks looking for donations. I quickly threw in a couple of dollars and went on my way. At this point, I didn't want any trouble, but the corruption was obvious.

I finally arrived in Ocho Rios and located Blue Mountain Hotel, but it was closed for renovations. I could not believe it. I traveled all this way, and the hotel was closed! Too bad someone, me included, did not think to call the hotel before sending me on a wild-goose chase. It was closed, but I would not be deterred.

I saw a security officer standing guard at the closed hotel. I explained my dilemma and explained that I needed to get in the hotel. I told him that I was a law enforcement officer and that I needed to get a picture of the inside for a trial back in the United States. Finally, I told him I would give him $200 for his trouble. He was looking at me skeptically until I mentioned the $200, and then he readily agreed to take me inside.

We entered the hotel, and I was hoping that the renovations had not disrupted the location where I needed to take the photo. I showed the security guard the photo and told him I needed to go near the pool. The guard immediately knew how to get to the pool and brought me to the exact location. I was even able to sit in the same chair Bernie was sitting in and took the same exact photo angle.

I thanked the security guard and handed him two crisp one-hundred-dollar bills. His eyes opened wide. That was probably a week's salary that he made in half an hour! He wanted to know where I was staying and offered to take me on a sightseeing trip. I was somewhat cautious; however, I agreed. He was a decent guy so far, and I figured he was somewhat reputable because he was a licensed security guard.

Later that afternoon, he picked me up at the hotel and took me for a ride in the country. We went to Dunn's River Falls and Park and walked through the falls. We stopped for lunch at a local outdoor restaurant and had jerk pork and Red Stripe beer. The locals were smoking ganja at the restaurant, and when that started, I told my guide we had to go.

He dropped me off at my hotel, and I gave him another one-hundred-dollar bill. I left Ocho Rios the next morning and drove back to Montego Bay and caught a flight to New York. While my trip was successful, the trial was over before I got back.

My trip and the information were not needed; however, as a young agent, I learned many things from this assignment. I learned how to work alone in a foreign country and how to be resourceful in order to complete the mission. The lessons learned from this trip served me well over the next twenty years.

As I previously stated, Bernie was convicted on all counts, including the credit card fraud. On July 3, 1984, he was sentenced to a twenty-six-year jail sentence. This was a harsh sentence for a financial crime but warranted in light of the crimes committed. Bernie was released from federal custody on August 30, 1991, after serving a seven-year sentence.

Both Bernie and Sam served significant jail time; however, both were lucky since they were sentenced before federal sentencing guidelines were introduced. If both were convicted after the new sentencing guidelines became law, they would have had to serve the full sentence as there is currently no parole in the federal system.

THE ARMORED CAR HEIST

I n November of 1986, while assigned to the Special Investigations Squad of the New York field office, I was assigned a bank larceny case—not as my usual role as an undercover agent but as case agent in charge of the investigation.

The case involved the theft of a shipment of cash from an armored car. A case of this nature was usually investigated by the Federal Bureau of Investigation (FBI), and Secret Service was rarely involved; however, since the shipment had a nexus to the Federal Reserve Bank of New York, Secret Service had jurisdiction in conjunction with the FBI.

I was assigned by the squad supervisor to attend a meeting at the Federal Reserve Bank of New York. I was advised that other attendees of the meeting would include bank security officials, agents from the FBI, and detectives from the New York Police Department (NYPD) and that we would receive a briefing on the theft.

I met with the bank officials and NYPD detectives; however, agents from the FBI did not attend the meeting. Their nonattendance would become an issue later. The bank security officials advised that on November 18, 1986, a $145,000 shipment of currency being transported by Loomis Armored Car Service to the Federal Reserve was missing $100,000 in $20 bills. The currency was part of a shipment being sent to the Federal Reserve for destruction as worn currency.

They advised that a canvas bag containing the currency was pried open, causing damage to the security seal, and that fifty packets of twenties totaling $100,000 was removed from the bag. The NYPD deferred investigation of the case to federal authorities, and since I was the only federal agent in the room, I took possession of the evidence, namely the canvas bag with the tampered seal, and started to conduct the investigation.

My theory for the FBI not showing up for the meeting and the NYPD deferring to federal authorities was that on face, this case was a very tough case to solve. Usually, in a theft of this type, employees working on the truck are involved; however, if the employee sticks to their story and claims no knowledge of the theft, it will be very hard to prove. Recently, there had been several high-profile cases of this type that were not solved for that reason. The difficulty of this type of case did not deter me, and as you will see, this case will have a very different outcome.

The following day, I drove out to Long Island City, Queens, to interview officials from Loomis Armored Car Service. I asked for the records from November 18, 1986, to identify who was working on the truck the day of the theft. The officials advised that the records of the trip were missing; however, they were able to identify the employees working.

The missing records were another indication that an employee was involved. They provided me the names of the driver and a second individual who rode in the front of the truck and the name of the third individual who rode in the back of the truck with the currency.

They further advised that the individual riding in the back of the truck, Richard Hamilton, had not reported for work since the day of the theft about three weeks ago. Additionally, they advised that Hamilton had not picked up two paychecks during that time. Subsequent investigation revealed that Hamilton was the suspect in a similar armored car theft on October 28, 1986, in Nassau County, Long Island. I didn't have to be Sherlock Holmes to figure out my prime suspect in the theft! I had some great circumstantial evidence, and now I had to prove it.

I drove to Hamilton's apartment on Harrison Avenue in the Bronx in an attempt to conduct an interview. The area was a high-crime area, and I took another agent with me for backup. Upon knocking on the door, we encountered Hamilton's girlfriend, Monica Jackson. We identified ourselves, and Jackson gave us a very apprehensive look and advised that Hamilton was not home. I asked her if we could come in to talk, and she agreed to let us in. Once inside, I was astonished at what we found.

Remember, we were in a very poor area of the Bronx, and Hamilton was a minimum-wage employee of an armored car company. Inside the apartment was about $3,000 worth of brand-new stereo equipment, a new large screen TV, and an expensive astronomer's telescope.

Plainly on the kitchen counter were receipts for the aforementioned items and receipts for $15,000 worth of jewelry. All items were purchased several days after the armored car theft. Jackson was even wearing some of the jewelry listed on the receipts. I had my man! Unless Hamilton was a recent lottery winner, he had a lot of explaining to do.

I called the field office and requested that several units respond to the apartment to secure the evidence and transport it to the field office, and I took possession of the receipts. I felt that we had enough evidence to seize the items and could not risk losing them by leaving and returning with a search warrant. I acted on the exigency of the situation, and as it turned out, that was the right call. Now we had to find Hamilton and the remainder of the cash.

For several days, I attempted to locate Hamilton, but he kept a low profile. Finally, he contacted me and agreed to be interviewed. I interviewed him at the field office, and after advising him of his Miranda rights, I explained the situation to him.

I told him that things did not look good for him. He did not show up for work the day after the theft, leaving two paychecks behind, and he purchased thousands of dollars of luxury items right after the theft. I told him now was the time to get in front of this, and if he cooperated in locating the missing money, his cooperation would be made known to federal prosecutors.

Hamilton agreed to cooperate and told the story of the theft. Hamilton stated that he stole the money by working loose the lead seal on the currency sack and removing fifty packets of $20 bills totaling $100,000 and then smuggling the cash off the truck in a personal bag. He also admitted to purchasing all the items that were seized from his apartment with the stolen money.

Hamilton stated that he paid a coworker, Donald Wilson, $2,000 to destroy the work records of the shipment in an attempt to cover up his involvement. He further advised that he gave $50,000 to his friend Eric McBride and asked him to hide it for him. Hamilton signed a sworn statement concerning these facts, and on December 12, 1986, he was arrested.

He appeared before a federal magistrate in the Eastern District of New York and was released on a $100,000 bond. Hamilton continued to cooperate in the investigation and helped locate McBride and recover the $50,000. Hamilton advised that McBride lived on Tremont Avenue in the Bronx, and Hamilton, another agent, and I headed to Tremont Avenue.

We were very lucky. Upon arrival, we spotted McBride leaving his apartment building and stopped him. Hamilton explained the situation to McBride, and McBride was fully cooperative. He acknowledged receiving the $50,000 from Hamilton; however, he stated he no longer had it. McBride stated that he became nervous holding the money and that he gave it to a third individual, William Arnold, who lived on Randall Avenue in the Bronx.

I called the field office and asked that they send additional units to meet us at Arnold's home on Randall Avenue. Upon arrival at Arnold's home, we confronted him with the situation, and he was fully cooperative. He acknowledged having the money and agreed to surrender it to us.

What happened next was pretty strange. Arnold took us to his backyard where he had a kennel with about twenty barking hunting dogs. It was a surreal sight. In the middle of the Bronx were all these hunting dogs caged neatly in rows behind a tenement building.

Arnold pointed to the cage where the money was hidden, which contained a nasty snarling dog. Neither I nor the other agents were going into the cage, so I told Arnold to go get it. Arnold went inside, retrieved a leather briefcase, and handed it to me. Upon inspection, the briefcase contained $49,800 in the stolen $20 bills.

We recovered a good portion of the stolen money, but where was the rest? We had about $20,000 in receipts and $49,800 in cash. That left $30,200 unaccounted for. I presented the facts to an assistant United States attorney in the Eastern District of New York and obtained arrest warrants for Wilson, McBride, and Arnold for conspiracy to commit bank larceny.

All were arrested on December 31, 1986, and all ultimately pled guilty to the charges; however, the missing $30,200 was never recovered. Hamilton ultimately spent two years in federal prison as a result of his crime. My bosses were very happy with the outcome of the case as was the armored car company.

We kept a low profile on the case so as not to embarrass the armored car company with the breach of security by one of their employees. However, January 1, 1987, must have been a slow news day, and an article regarding the theft and arrests was published in the *New York Daily News*.

I was mentioned in the article, and the article even went into detail about the money being recovered from a dog pen full of barking dogs. Several days after the article was published, I received a call from an FBI supervisor from their New York field office. The supervisor wanted to know why I got involved in a bank larceny case. He was being kind of a jerk, so I let him have it.

I told him that his agents were irresponsible for not showing up for the initial meeting at the Federal Reserve Bank. I told him that Secret Service clearly had jurisdiction since there was a nexus to the Federal Reserve and that his problem should not be with me but with the FBI agents who dropped the ball on this one. I told him not to call me again and that if he still had a problem, he should call my supervisor. I never heard anything about it again.

THE LONG SHOT

I opened the hallway closet door, and inside was my backup Billy McGee holding a short-barreled Remington 870 shotgun. He had this intense look on his face, and sweat was dripping down his head.

"Hey, Billy. If things break bad in here, make sure I'm out of the line of fire when you come out of the door."

"No problem, Tommy. I got your back," he said.

Billy was an intense guy, and I wanted to make sure that I was not collateral damage if this deal should go bad, which, given the situation, was a strong possibility.

The late 1980s brought the country the savings and loan scandals. Insiders and others at these local banking institutions committed frauds, which caused an epidemic of bank failures throughout the country. Legislative action was taken in Congress, giving Secret Service concurrent jurisdiction with the FBI to investigate violations of federal bank fraud laws.

The FBI was not too happy about the Secret Service being granted this authority, but Congress felt differently. After the Scarpa case and my time in the fraud squad, I was transferred to the Special Investigations Squad and appointed as the Organized Crime Strike Force representative to the Eastern District of New York US Attorney's Office.

This Special Investigations Squad was responsible for inv gating bank fraud cases as well as frauds and thefts related to U Treasury bonds and securities. In the spirit of cooperation, I was assigned to the FBI bank fraud task force and reported directly to office space that I was assigned at the FBI New York field office. Given my past experience with the FBI in the Scarpa case, I was not too happy about the assignment, but I followed my orders and tried to make it work.

The task force consisted of members of the FBI, NYPD, and me, the lone Secret Service agent. It was not a great working relation- ship as the NYPD detectives, and I found ourselves excluded from many meetings held by the FBI squad members. I got the feeling that the FBI supervisors were not too happy that I was assigned to the task force and were not keeping me in the loop on many issues.

Having been an agent for several years and after being burned by the FBI on the Scarpa case, I knew that this was how they did business. It was well-known throughout the law enforcement com- munity that the FBI would take any information that you could pro- vide but would not be forthcoming with information that would help another agency's case.

In the summer of 1987, I was sitting at the FBI task force when I received a call from Special Investigations Squad backup Mike Singer.

"Hey, Tommy. We are setting up a deal to buy stolen bonds. We need you to do the undercover. Head back to the field office," he said.

What a relief. I was at my boiling point dealing with the FBI, and getting out of there for a while was just what I needed. Doing an undercover deal was even better as this was my favorite part of the job. Little did I know what I was getting myself into. To repay the favor, I made sure that I didn't tell my FBI counterparts what was going on!

At the office, I met with squad supervisor Nick Lester and squad backup Singer. They explained that they had an informant who had information on an individual who was trying to sell $100,000 in y securities and that I would do the undercover

s for the informant to introduce me to the target
Harlem. I thought for a moment about what was
ig a native New Yorker, the word *Harlem*, which
can American neighborhood, made me think.

"Harlem?" I exclaimed. "Is the target black?"

The first rule of undercover work was that a black guy should deal with a black undercover, a white guy should deal with a white undercover, etc. Using individuals from similar backgrounds helped build trust, which led to more successful undercover operations. Trying to set me up for an undercover meeting in Harlem was unorthodox, to say the least, and the possibility of putting me in a dangerous situation at worst.

"Yes, the informant and target are black," said Lester.

"If that's the case, why am I doing the undercover?" I asked. Most of my past undercover assignments were with white guys, usually of Irish or Italian descent, and I felt a little uncomfortable with the scenario that was being presented to me.

"We don't have anyone else, and this is too big of a case to pass up," said Singer. The New York field office of the 1980s was not as diverse as it is today, and there were few African American agents available to do this deal.

"Okay, Mike, I'll do it," I said, "but I want to do it my way. Completing this deal is a long shot, and I want to make sure no one gets hurt, especially me."

The next day, I met with the confidential informant, Willie, at the New York field office. Willie explained that a guy whom he knew from the neighborhood named Rico had $100,000.00 in stolen US savings bonds that he wanted to sell.

Willie stated that Rico was a small-time criminal who obtained the bonds in a burglary of a Westchester County home. I asked for some background on Rico, and Willie provided a physical description and said that he hung out at a bodega on 128th Street and St. Nicholas Avenue. However, he could not provide a vehicle or residence for Rico.

I asked if Rico carried a gun, was involved in violent criminal activity, or addicted to drugs. Willie advised that he did not know if he carried a gun or of any past violent criminal activity; however, he did say that Rico did smoke a lot of weed. I asked the informant how Rico might react to meeting a white guy to purchase the bonds. The informant looked surprised.

"A white guy?" he exclaimed. "Not too many white guys taking care of business on St. Nick. May not work."

"Well, if this deal is going to go down, I'm the guy that's going to meet him," I said.

The informant, who was motivated by the money he would be paid by Secret Service, changed his tune and suggested that he would set up a meeting between me and Rico at his apartment, which was at 127th Street and 8th Avenue in Harlem.

"You're a New York guy. He may deal with you, but we should keep it off the street," he said. "I will set up a meeting at my apartment. It will attract a lot less attention than meeting on St. Nick."

I advised the informant that doing the deal at his apartment might put him in a bad position with Rico once we arrested him. The informant advised that he was not worried about Rico and that he would deal with him if he had to. At this point, the informant was totally motivated by greed and the $5,000 reward he would be paid if the bonds were recovered.

I told him to reach out to Rico and set up a meeting with me for some time this week, giving us at least twenty-four hours' notice so that we had time to prepare for the meet. I told him to tell Rico that I was an Italian wise guy from Brooklyn with connections at a bank that would be able to cash the bonds. I also told him to say that I would pay him cash up front for the bonds.

Again, I asked the informant if he was comfortable doing the deal at his apartment, and he said he was. I could see the dollar signs in his eyes. He was more focused on the reward than on how this could come back on him when we arrested Rico.

Willie contacted me the next day and said he set the meeting with Rico in two days at three o'clock in the afternoon this Friday at his apartment. He said that he told Rico my cover story and that

Rico was somewhat apprehensive but eventually agreed to meet with me. I told Willie to go to the bodega where Rico hung out that afternoon and engage him in conversation outside the store.

A surveillance van was sent up at the bodega with agents who were familiar with the informant in an attempt to get photographs of Rico while they met. Additionally, another two agents were sent to the area in an attempt to surveil Rico to a residence. Later that afternoon, the surveillance van was able to get photos of Rico while he met with Willie.

After their meeting, Rico left the bodega in a livery cab, and the other surveillance team was able to follow him to an apartment building on West 187th Street in Washington Heights where the George Washington Bridge entered Manhattan. We got lucky. We were able to get a photograph of the target and a possible residence for him.

A squad briefing was scheduled for 8:00 a.m. on Friday to set an operational plan for my undercover meeting. I went to the informant's apartment on Thursday to look at the layout. It was a one-bedroom ground floor apartment with a kitchen and a living room. The ground floor was ideal as covering teams would be able to respond to the apartment quickly should there be a problem.

At the Friday morning briefing, we discussed what information we had on Rico and came to the realization that there were still some missing pieces. We knew what he looked like and had a possible residence for him, but we knew nothing about his past criminal activity or his propensity for violence.

As the undercover agent, I agreed with those concerns along with my initial concern about the scenario of Rico dealing with a white guy in Harlem, which went against the rules of undercover work. To alleviate those concerns and mitigate the risk to me, it was decided to put a covering agent in the apartment with me. The agent would be positioned in a hallway closet adjacent to the living room where he would be in a position to respond should the need arise. The agent assigned was Billy McGee.

McGee and I arrived at the informant's apartment on Friday afternoon several hours prior to the scheduled meeting with Rico.

McGee brought a short-barreled Remington 870 shotgun for extra firepower and cleared space in the closet. Several teams of agents were discretely stationed outside to observe Rico arrive and to cover the deal. I had about $500 in flash money to show Rico, if necessary, but I had no intention of paying him. I would be wearing a wire transmitter, and once I saw the bonds, I would give the prearranged signal "Acapulco" over the transmitter and the covering teams would move in for the arrest. The apartment door would be conveniently left open by the informant Willie.

At 2:30 p.m., one of the covering teams observed Rico walking down the block toward the informant's apartment and advised me by radio. McGee shut off the radio and took his position in the closet. Everything was set. Twenty minutes after the initial notification, Rico had still not arrived at the apartment. I checked on McGee in the closet to see how he was doing.

McGee was standing there with the shotgun and an intense look on his face and was sweating profusely. The sweat was dripping down his forehead, and he looked ready for action. I became a little concerned that if something happened, he would come out blasting, and I might be in the line of fire. I reminded him of that, and he said he had everything under control. "I know you do, but I'm just reminding you. I don't want to wind up in the hospital today."

Normally, I wouldn't remind an agent about something like that, but the intense look on his face while clutching the shotgun made me say something. The covering agents advised us by radio that Rico was on the block, talking to an individual, and then advised that he was making his way toward the informant's apartment.

About ten minutes later, Rico knocked on the door and was let in the apartment by the informant. The informant introduced me to Rico.

"Hey, Rico. This is my boy Tommy, the guy I told you about. He's with the Italian crew in Brooklyn."

Rico looked me over for a minute and didn't say a word. I extended my hand to Rico and said, "Hey, how are you doing?"

Rico didn't respond to my gesture and just stared at me with a scowl on his face. Finally, he said to me, "What are you doing up here? You're a long way from Brooklyn. You could get yourself in trouble in Harlem."

I began to get an uneasy feeling about Rico. I responded, "I am here to make some money. I really don't care where I make it. Money is money whether in Brooklyn or Harlem. It's all green. Are you here to make some money, or do you just want to bullshit with me?" I said.

Rico didn't respond. I could tell he was getting nervous and that he didn't like my response. I continued the conversation. "And by the way, I'm not going to get myself in trouble in Harlem. I've done deals here before, and I know how it works here."

My worst fears had come true. Sending me to do an undercover deal in Harlem was a mistake, and now I had to deal with a very nervous target with a potential to break bad on me.

"Are you ready to make some money? Did you bring the bonds?" I asked Rico.

Again, he looked at me with a scowl and said, "Hey, man, I don't know what you are talking about."

I turned to the informant and said, "I thought this guy was all right? Now he's wasting my time. What's going on?"

The informant turned to Rico and said, "Hey, man. My boy Tommy is good. Everything is cool."

Rico responded, "No, it's not. I think you boy is a cop."

For the first time in all my undercover assignments, I was made as a cop, and now I had to deal with a potentially volatile situation, not to mention a tense covering agent in the closet with a shotgun. The best way to deal with the accusation of being a cop during an undercover meeting is to turn the table on the target and accuse them of being a cop.

"How do I know you are not a cop?" I asked Rico. He just stared at me and did not respond. "I know you are not a cop because my man Willie vouched for you, and my man Willie is vouching for me. That's how it works. Do you have a problem with Willie?" I asked.

The situation was getting very tense. My adrenaline was pumping, and I watched every gesture and facial expression of Rico to try to determine his next move. Finally, Rico responded and said, "I got a problem with you. You are a cop."

I was going to try to keep the conversation going, but as Rico finished his sentence, he quickly reached into his jacket pocket. Based on how badly the conversation was going and his abrupt move, I instinctively drew my .38 revolver from my waistband and pointed it at Rico's chest.

"Slowly take your hand out of your pocket and place both hands on the table," I shouted. As I was shouting, my covering agent burst from his hiding place in the closet and pointed the shotgun at Rico. Rico appeared stunned at suddenly having two guns pointed at him and complied with my order.

"Hey, man, what are you doing?" he shouted.

"I'm just protecting myself," I said. "You called me a cop and then reached into your pocket. What do you have in there?" I asked.

Billy McGee reached into Rico's pocket and pulled out an Iver Johnson .22 pistol. My instincts were right. Things were about to break bad, and I reacted in the right way.

"You are right, I am a cop, and now you are under arrest."

McGee searched and handcuffed Rico, and I handcuffed Willie. Willie was arrested also to try to cover him from being the informant who set Rico up. It wouldn't take a rocket scientist to figure out what happened, but it was the best we could do to cover him at the time.

The surveillance agents moved in and transported Rico and Willie back to the New York field office. Unfortunately, Rico did not have the stolen bonds on him; however, he did have an illegal gun, and the NYPD was more than willing to take custody of him and charge him in state court. Rico eventually pleaded guilty and spent time in state prison.

I learned a lot from this deal. Primarily, I learned that if a situation did not feel right, don't do the deal. I was uncomfortable with the scenario in Harlem, but did it anyway because an African American agent was unavailable. I was put in a dangerous situation as well as my covering agent and the informant. Luckily, no one was shot, but it could have very easily happened. Live and learn.

My September 1983 graduation from special agent training in Beltsville, Maryland. Presenting my graduation certificate is the late, former Director, John R. Simpson.

The badge carried by Secret Service special
agents during the 1980's and 1990's.

Surveillance photo of "Tommy Ferraro" on his way to
meet Greg "the Grim Reaper" Scarpa at the Wimpy
Boys Social Club, Dyker Heights, Brooklyn.

The armored car heist investigation resulted in the recovery of $49,800 of $100,000 stolen by an employee of the company. The money was found hidden in a dog kennel in the Bronx. Five individuals were subsequently arrested for the theft. (The other Secret Service employees in the photo are redacted for privacy concerns.)

ARMORED CAR GUARDS CHARGED

100G theft bared

By DANIEL HAYS
Daily News Staff Writer

Two armored car guards were charged yesterday with filching $100,000 in cash that was bound for the federal government's used-money furnace. They stashed the loot in a kennel full of yapping dogs in the Bronx, but federal agents sniffed it out.

Charged in Brooklyn Federal Court with conspiracy to commit bank larceny are Donald Wilson, 22, of Astoria Blvd. in Queens, and Robert Hamilton, 20, of Harrison Ave. in the Bronx. Both worked for Loomis Armored Car Co. of Long Island City.

Also charged are Eric McBride and William Arnold, both Bronx men who allegedly helped hide the loot, and Hamilton's live-in girl friend, Monica Jackson, 22.

Part of 145G load

According to court records, Hamilton was guarding $145,000 in used cash that was being shipped on Nov. 18 from a Queens bank to the Federal Reserve Bank in Manhattan for destruction.

He allegedly worked loose a lead seal on the money sack and removed 50 packets of $20 bills—$100,000—then smuggled the cash off the truck in his personal bag.

That was Hamilton's last day on the job. When Secret Service Agent Thomas Farrell found Hamilton at his Bronx home a month later, he found receipts from a $20,000 shopping spree.

Farrell said Hamilton admitted he paid co-worker Wilson $2,000 to destroy work records for the day of the theft. Hamilton said he gave $50,000 to McBride, who led agents to the Randall Ave. home of Arnold.

Nearby, federal agents found a kennel filled with dozens of barking dogs—and a briefcase holding $49,800 in cash. About $30,000 is unaccounted for, and Arnold is on the lam, authorities said.

Gov judges 'em fit to promote

Gov. Cuomo yesterday named two Supreme Court justices to the Appellate Division and redesignated two justices of the mid-level appeals court to new terms.

George Bundy Smith, 49, a state Supreme Court justice in Manhattan, was assigned to the First Department of the Appellate Division, covering Manhattan and the Bronx. Smith replaces Justice Arnold Fein, whose term expired.

Cuomo also designated Reuben Davis, 65, of Rochester, to the Fourth Department in western New York.

Cuomo also announced the redesignation of Associate Justice Joseph Sullivan to the First Department and Justice Moses Weinstein to the Second Department, which includes Brooklyn, Staten Island, Long Island and the northern suburbs of New York City.

All of the judges are elected and the designations are not subject to confirmation by the Legislature.

Execs flee fire

A fire in an executive dining room in a Financial District skyscraper housing offices of Drexel Burnham Lambert Inc. forced the evacuation of the two top floors of the 40-story tower.

One man forced to walk down 31 floors to safety complained of chest pains, but no other injuries were reported in the fire at 60 Broad St.

It must have been a slow news day in the Big Apple! On January 1, 1987, an article concerning the theft appeared in the NY Daily News.

WANTED

by the
United States Secret Service

Domingo "Miguel" Pimentel

For the murder of a Government Witness   J-108-711-203912-S

Race: Dominican
Sex: Male
Date of Birth: 11/2/52
Height: 5' 6"
Weight: 140 lbs.
Hair: Black
Eyes: Brown

FBI No. 140321M2
SSN: 085-50-0175
Last Known Address:
    1261 Merriam Ave.
    Bronx, NY

AKA: Miguel Pimentel

Other Info: Wanted by the United States Secret Service for the murder of a Government Witness. Cash Reward Available.

If you have any information on this individual please contact the New York Field Office of the U.S. Secret Service at: 212-466-4400, 24 hours a day.

Wanted Poster of Domingo Pimentel for the murder of a government witness in a counterfeiting case. Pimentel was a fugitive for two years before finally being apprehended by Secret Service agents in San Juan, Puerto Rico. Pimentel was convicted at trial and received a sentence of life without parole.

Not in my "Street Guy" mode. Taking a break from undercover work protecting President Ronald Reagan and Mrs. Reagan. The photograph was taken aboard the aircraft carrier USS John F. Kennedy during the centennial celebration of the Statue of Liberty on July 4, 1986.

After my undercover work in the New York field office, I spent five years in headquarters and on the Vice Presidential Protective Division. Protection afforded me the opportunity to travel to some great places and witness historical events, but "Street Guy" couldn't wait to get back on the street! This photo is circa 1993 while protecting Vice President Al Gore.

"Tommy Ferraro" in Baltimore's Little Italy setting up a counterfeit currency deal with three wise guys from Phoenix, AZ. There is $5,000,000 in counterfeit US currency in the trunk of the Mustang.

Tempting fate! Playing with tigers while assigned to the counterfeiting task force in Bangkok, Thailand.

Another wildlife encounter while assigned to the task force in Thailand.

MURDER IN THE BRONX

In the late 1980s, living in New York City was like living in the Wild West. The murder rate was skyrocketing, much of it fueled by the crack cocaine epidemic. In 1988 and 1989, there were nearly 2,000 murders in the city with a peak of nearly 2,300 in 1991.

Against this backdrop of murder and drug trafficking, the counterfeiting of US currency was widespread throughout the city. The Russians in Brighton Beach, Brooklyn, the Colombians in Corona, Queens, and the Dominicans in Washington Heights, Manhattan, all had extensive counterfeiting operations.

I spent two years in the New York field office counterfeit squad, investigating and arresting bad actors from all three groups. Counterfeit notes produced by those criminal organizations are etched in my memory. Secret Service analyzed these various notes by printing characteristics, defects in the currency image, and paper quality. This analysis would link specific notes to particular printers and criminal organizations.

Any agent who worked in the counterfeit squad during this time will never forget the long days and nights spent chasing down leads of these notes. It was the high watermark of counterfeiting in New York City, and I was glad to be part of it.

During this time, the counterfeit was produced using the photo offset process—that is, taking a photo of a genuine note, transferring the photo image into a plate, and producing the note on an offset printing press. The Colombians did even better. They manufactured an engraved plate rather than a photo offset plate, which produced a very high-quality counterfeit note.

Engraving took skill and was similar to the way the US Treasury manufactured genuine currency. In about a decade, with the advent of computer technology and desktop publishing software, most counterfeit would be manufactured using a computer in someone's living room or dorm room. My time in the New York counterfeit squad was truly the end of an era.

The following case is just one story but one that had serious consequences. It was a simple buy bust that turned deadly. I was not an undercover agent in this case but part of a large team.

As previously stated, the Colombian note was a high-quality one-hundred-dollar bill, which was being passed all over the city. Naturally, when we had someone who had information on the note, it was a top priority.

Juan Andres Guerrero Gonzalez was an informant developed by an agent in the squad who had such information. Andres knew an individual in the Bronx named Miguel and his wife, Ronna, who were sources of counterfeit currency. Andres, as he was known, agreed to set up a deal and purchase the counterfeit from Miguel and Ronna.

The ultimate goal of a counterfeiting investigation is the seizure of the manufacturing plant, specifically, the printing press and plates. This is accomplished by making purchases of counterfeit currency, arresting that individual, and obtaining their cooperation in making a purchase from their source. The goal is to repeat this process and work your way back to the printer. This process is not always successful but is the best way to get to the printer.

On August 9, 1988, Andres met with Miguel and Ronna, who were later identified as Domingo Miguel Pimentel and his common-law wife, Ronna Deziel, in Joyce Kilmer Park in the Bronx. Andres purchased $5,000 in counterfeit currency for $1,000 in genuine currency provided by Secret Service.

The deal was a buy through. We let Pimentel and Deziel go after the purchase in order to build up trust between them and Andres with the goal of making a much larger purchase. A second meeting was set up for August 12, 1988, again at Joyce Kilmer Park in the Bronx. Andres met with Pimentel and Deziel and purchased another package of counterfeit. This deal, however, was a buy bust, and when Andres gave a prearranged signal, arrest teams moved in and arrested Pimentel and Deziel.

A search incident to arrest the couples' car uncovered an additional $105,000 in counterfeit. It was a great seizure and an indication that Pimentel and Deziel were close to the printer. Mike Mullin and I transported Pimentel to the New York field office for processing and interview. Along the way, Pimentel became enraged and started cursing, spitting, and kicking in the back seat of the vehicle.

We had to pull into the parking lot of the McDonald's near the Third Avenue Bridge and talk to Pimentel about showing proper respect to federal agents and government vehicles. He was quiet for the rest of the trip; however, I knew we were dealing with a very bad dude with this guy. We would soon find out how vicious he was.

Upon arrival at the field office, Pimentel and Deziel were processed and interviewed. Both declined to provide any information and were lodged in the Metropolitan Correctional Center pending an initial appearance before a federal magistrate.

Mullin and I went to the US Attorney's Office for the Southern District of New York and drafted complaints for Pimentel and Deziel. Both appeared before the magistrate and were held pending a bail review. By the way the complaint was written, it was pretty obvious who was providing information to the government. Even before he saw the complaint, by the way the arrest went down, I was sure Pimentel was thinking that Andres had set him up.

On September 7, 1988, both Pimentel and Deziel were released on bail. They were residents of Rhode Island, and the conditions of their bail permitted them to travel between the Southern District of New York and their home. On November 1, 1988, both pleaded guilty to dealing in counterfeit obligations of the United States in violation of 18 USC 473, and both faced decades in jail. Sentencing was set for January 4, 1989. Pimentel would never appear for that sentencing, and the situation was about to become much worse.

Testimony later revealed that immediately after Pimentel and Deziel's arrest, Pimentel suspected that Andres was a snitch and stated that he would kill him if he ever found him. At that time, Pimentel and other relatives began scouring the Bronx neighborhood where they believed Andres lived.

On November 2, 1988, a day after he pleaded guilty to the counterfeiting charge, Pimentel found Andres on Merriam Avenue in the Bronx, a block where Pimentel's relatives lived. Andres was talking to a woman in front of 1304 Merriam Avenue, and in full view of numerous witnesses, Pimentel did the unthinkable.

Witnesses later confirmed that Pimentel retrieved a red-and-yellow baseball bat from the trunk of a car of an individual he knew, and with the bat behind his back, he walked up the hill toward 1304 Merriam Avenue. According to the witness, Pimentel ran up behind Andres, took a batter's stance, and struck Andres in the back of the head with the baseball bat.

As the witness heard the bat smashing into Andres's skull, she saw Andres turn and fall to the ground, his hands never leaving his pockets. The witness stated that Pimentel stood over the body of Andres and continued to smash his head with the bat fifteen to twenty times. Pimentel fled the scene, throwing the bat into a vacant lot on Merriam Avenue.

Through information provided by witnesses, the bat was recovered later by agents of the New York field office. Several minutes after the assault, officers from the NYPD and paramedics arrived on the scene. Andres was transported to the hospital where he was pronounced dead later that evening.

The effects of the attack were horrific. An assistant New York City medical examiner later testified that virtually every bone in Andres's face and skull was shattered as a result of the assault and that the injuries were consistent with blows from a baseball bat. His was a young life cut short by the act of an animal.

Pimentel and Deziel returned to Rhode Island on the evening of the murder. They were together for about a week until Pimentel suddenly disappeared. Pimentel left Rhode Island and returned to his native Dominican Republic. At the time, the United States and the Dominican Republic did not have an extradition treaty, and Pimentel felt safe from the reach of the United States judicial system.

Pimentel became a most wanted fugitive of Secret Service, and agents in our field office in San Juan, Puerto Rico, developed informants in the Dominican Republic to track his movements. Through contacts in the US Customs and informants in the Dominican Republic, attempts were made to lure Pimentel out of the Dominican Republic to a gambling junket on a boat offshore.

Once offshore, he would be arrested by federal agents and the US Coast Guard; however, the attempts at this were unsuccessful. The Service was frustrated but never relented in their attempts to capture Pimentel. Finally, Pimentel made a mistake. He left the safety of the Dominican Republic and traveled to Puerto Rico.

Informants in the Dominican Republic quickly notified the San Juan field office of his movement, and on June 22, 1990, Pimentel was arrested by agents of the San Juan field office at a pool hall in San Juan. Initially, Pimentel thought the agents were from the Immigration and Naturalization Service and had a very cocky attitude. However, once he realized they were agents from Secret Service, he became very dejected and fearful.

The fear of arrest overcame him. He knew he would be spending the rest of his life in jail. Pimentel was extradited to the Southern District of New York. On August 2, 1991, after a five-day trial, Pimentel was convicted of the murder of Andres. He was subsequently sentenced to life imprisonment.

It was a bittersweet victory for Secret Service. We took a dangerous criminal off the street, but a young man with a long life ahead of him had all his dreams shattered in one horrific, violent act. On a personal note, Andres was killed on my second wedding anniversary. For the past thirty years, when I celebrate my anniversary, I think about a tragic loss of life that occurred on a street in the Bronx many years ago.

As of this writing, Domingo Pimentel is incarcerated in the Federal Correction Institute, Edgefield, South Carolina, under a sentence of life. He is sixty-six years old and will never see the outside of a federal prison.

THE LAST DEAL

After spending six and a half years in the New York field office, I was promoted and transferred to a headquarters position in Washington, DC, at the Special Investigations and Security Division. It was a desk job that I didn't really relish, but it was a promotion and a good career move.

My life had changed since I started in the New York office. I got married, and my wife, Christina, and I now had an eleven-month-old son. We purchased a condo in New Jersey and were now preparing for a family move to Maryland. There was much to do. We had to sell our condo, look for a house in Maryland, and prepare to have all our belongings transported to Maryland. As you can imagine, there was a lot going on in the Farrell household.

Against the backdrop of the impending move, I was still working in the field office. I was assigned to the counterfeit squad, and we were very busy with the many criminal groups—such as the Russians, Colombians, and Dominicans—manufacturing and passing counterfeit US currency throughout New York City.

Wednesday, November 29, 1989, was my last day in the New York field office. The movers were coming the following day to pack my belongings, and on Friday morning, we would be on our way to Maryland. I expected to have a quiet day in the office, turn in my equipment and vehicle, and get a ride home from one of the guys in the office. However, the supervisor in the counterfeit squad had other ideas.

A reliable confidential source came to the office that morning with a sample of counterfeit currency and claimed that he would be able to introduce an undercover agent to the source to make a purchase of a large quantity. The squad supervisor stopped by my desk.

"Hey, Tommy. We need you to do the undercover on this one." I couldn't believe it. My last day in the office and he was asking me to do an undercover deal.

"Boss, you know that today is my last day. I'm off to Maryland on Friday."

"Yeah, I know, but the counterfeit note is the Colombian note, and we really need to make this deal work. That note has been killing us. You know that. You are the guy who can get the deal done."

He was right, the Colombian note was a hot note, and buying a large package could point us in the direction of a major player. So as a good soldier, as the expression goes, I agreed to do the undercover assignment. I went to the interview room and met with the informant.

He advised that he received the counterfeit samples from a guy named Tony who frequented the area of Thirty-Ninth Street and Fifth Avenue in the Sunset Park section of Brooklyn. He advised that Tony had a large package that he was trying to sell.

I asked the usual questions: "What does Tony look like?" "Does he carry a firearm?" "How long have you known him?" "What other criminal activity is he involved with?" "How do you contact him?" After about a half hour of interviewing, the confidential source painted a picture of Tony.

To me, Tony appeared to be a street hustler who was out to make a quick buck any way he could. The confidential source described Tony as Italian, in his early twenties, about five foot eleven, and 180 pounds. He fitted the description of one thousand wise guys in that neighborhood! I had dealt with many individuals like him through the years.

According to the confidential source, Tony did not carry a firearm; but for my safety, I would deal with him as if he did. The confidential source said he had Tony's home phone number and that he could call him to set up a meeting with me for later that afternoon. Through that phone number, we were able to obtain an address for Tony.

The informant called Tony from an undercover telephone line in the office, and I recorded the call. I instructed the confidential source to order a package of $10,000 in the counterfeit note and to tell Tony that the buyer was willing to pay twenty points, or 20 percent, of face value for it. I told him to tell Tony that the buyer wanted to do the deal directly with him. And that he did not want anyone else to handle his $2,000 in cash.

Criminals did not like to talk directly about criminal activity on the phone, so when Tony answered the phone, he said he would call him back from a pay phone, and the confidential source gave him the undercover line telephone number.

Prior to the phone call, I told the confidential source to set my meeting with Tony at the corner of Thirty-Ninth Street and Fifth Avenue, a location that Tony was very familiar with and that he would feel comfortable meeting me at. There was a luncheonette on the corner, and I would meet him by it.

I picked the location because it was a very busy corner. It was the intersection of two New York City bus lines, and there were bus stops on both streets. During the day, there was a lot of vehicle and pedestrian traffic. I felt that the busy location would be good to mitigate the chance of a rip-off just in case Tony was thinking about going down that road. It would also be a good location for my covering teams to blend in as they watched my back. I was on my way to Maryland, and the last thing I needed was to have a problem on my last day and last deal in the Big Apple!

Tony called back from a pay phone about fifteen minutes later. After a painfully cryptic phone call—again, street guys don't like to talk on the phone—finally, the meeting was set. The confidential source told Tony that I would meet him by the luncheonette on the corner of Thirty-Ninth Street and Fifth Avenue at 2:00 p.m. that afternoon. He gave Tony my description and name and told him I would be driving a tan Cadillac DeVille.

The deal was set, but I began to wonder. The deal was put together too easily, and Tony readily agreed to meet me. Either he really trusted the confidential source or he was not as streetwise as I thought. Or perhaps Tony had planned to rip me off from the beginning and I was being targeted for a $2,000 robbery.

I could live with the first two scenarios, but I would make sure the third scenario never happened. I would be armed to protect myself; I would be wired so my covering team would hear what was going on; and I would be covered by some of the best in the business.

I felt very confident going to the meet. Several covering units were dispatched to the meet location, and the transmitter and monitor were tested to ensure that the covering agents could monitor and record my conversations. Once the covering units were in place, I left the field office in the undercover Cadillac for the twenty-minute drive to the meeting location. The covering units checked in and advised that they had not seen the suspect Tony in the vicinity of the meet location.

I was about four blocks from the meeting location, waiting for a traffic light, when someone opened my passenger door and jumped in. I was startled and turned toward the guy and realized it was Tony.

"Hey, Tommy. I saw the Caddy and knew it was you. How are you doing?"

"How am I doing?" I said. "Not too fucking good. Now get out of my car. You were told I would meet you by the luncheonette on Fifth Avenue. What the fuck are you doing here?"

"Hey, man, relax," he said. "I was on my way over there and saw you driving by and just thought I would get things moving."

"I don't know you, and it don't work like that," I said. "Now get out, and I'll meet you on Fifth Avenue. That was the agreement."

Tony gave me a quizzical look and left my vehicle. That was a close call. Had Tony planned on robbing me of the buy money, he could have gotten the drop on me when he jumped in the vehicle or, worse, put a bullet in me. At least I knew that there was less of a chance of a robbery now since he quickly left my vehicle.

Hopefully, by my reaction, I didn't scare him away, but I had to react that way. I did not want to do the deal away from my covering teams, and to save battery life, I had not even turned on my transmitter. I would have been totally uncovered and on my own. So much for driving with my doors unlocked. Lesson learned!

I quickly drove away in the opposite direction of Tony and contacted the covering teams by the radio hidden in the glove box of the Caddy. I advised them of what had happened and gave them a description of Tony and told them to let me know when he arrived in the vicinity of the luncheonette. To avoid any more issues, I was not heading that way until I knew he was at the agreed meeting location.

About fifteen minutes later, one of the covering units radioed and said that Tony was outside the luncheonette. "Great, I didn't scare him away." I turned on and tested my transmitter and advised the covering agents that I was headed over to meet Tony. I then shut off my radio.

Upon arrival at the luncheonette, I saw Tony standing outside and motioned for him to get in the vehicle. I planned on doing the deal right there and shut off the vehicle. Tony jumped in and said, "Hey, man, why did you get so pissed off back there?"

I responded, "I didn't know who the hell you were, and you just jumped in my car. Like I said, I don't do business like that. If you are here to deal, let's see what you got," I said.

I cautiously watched as Tony pulled a package from under his shirt. He handed it to me. It was a neat stack of one hundred crisp counterfeit one-hundred-dollar bills, and it was the Colombian note. After reviewing the package, I placed it under the front seat of the vehicle. "I'll be right back," I said. "Your cash is in the trunk." The prearranged signal to my covering team was opening the trunk of my vehicle. Once opened, the team would move in and arrest me and Tony.

I exited the vehicle, opened the trunk, and waited for the team to move in. I was standing for what felt like an eternity, and no one showed up at the vehicle. I had a problem. While I picked that location for the deal because of its pedestrian and vehicle traffic, that same traffic had created my problem. When I exited the vehicle to open the trunk, traffic had built up at the red light at the corner. A large New York City bus was stopped alongside my vehicle, blocking the view of my vehicle from the covering team. While they heard me exit the vehicle through the transmitter, no one actually saw the open trunk.

I looked inside the vehicle and saw Tony nervously fidgeting in the front seat. Where was my covering team? I was sure they were on the way. Suddenly, Tony exited the vehicle. "Hey, man, what's going on? Where is my money?" I looked at him and didn't respond, and he made a sudden threatening move toward me. I instinctively drew my .38 revolver from my waistband, leveled it at Tony, and identified myself as a federal agent.

Tony stopped in his tracks and then suddenly bolted like a rabbit down Fifth Avenue. Luckily, he ran right into two of the covering agents responding to my vehicle, who quickly took him down and put him in handcuffs. That was the second time I had to draw my weapon during an undercover deal, and I was not happy with it.

What should have been a routine buy bust got complicated and dangerous—first, when the target suddenly jumped in my vehicle and, second, when I had to draw my weapon. Someone could have gotten hurt. We were lucky that day. My last deal could have been a disaster.

The deal with Tony worked out as planned. Facing charges of a hand-to-hand transaction with a federal agent, he decided to cooperate. His cooperation led to seizures of hundreds of thousands of dollars of the Colombian note. I never dealt with the Colombian note again.

I left New York two days later for my assignment in Washington, DC. For the next five years, I would be working in headquarters and on the Vice Presidential Protective Division. I would be far from the streets of New York and the undercover work I loved. It would be six years before I would have the adrenaline rush of working undercover again.

AGENT PROVOCATEUR

I hopped into a taxi and headed to the railway station in Tampere, Finland. My heart was racing, and I was anxious to get away from the hotel as quickly as possible. I had just purchased a package of counterfeit currency and did not want to be followed by the criminals I had just met with. My counterparts from the National Bureau of Investigation (NBI) would be following close behind to ensure my safety.

I quickly exited the taxi and raced up the steps of the railway station with my adrenaline pumping. As I opened the door and entered, I came face-to-face with a uniformed Finnish police officer. He looked at me, and I could tell he was wondering who I was. I was dressed like a New York wise guy, pinky ring and all, and I just didn't fit into this quiet town in the Finnish countryside.

As he looked me over, I made a quick right and headed to the restroom. I began to process the situation and realized that if he stopped me, I would have a major problem. I had $10,000 in counterfeit US currency in my pocket and a .38 revolver in my waistband.

Under Finnish law, if the officer found the gun and counterfeit currency, I could be charged with a crime, and my NBI counterparts would have a lot of explaining to do. I would be responsible for creating an international incident!

I entered the restroom, headed for a stall, and locked the door behind me. I sat there with my heart pounding, hoping the officer did not follow me into the restroom.

In early 1996, the United States government redesigned the familiar look of the US dollar for the first time since the 1920s. This redesign was an attempt to thwart counterfeiting, which had reached epidemic proportions in the mid-1990s.

The advent of computer technology, desktop publishing software, and quality printers made counterfeiting possible to anyone with a computer. Also, the dollarization of many foreign currencies made the dollar a very tempting target for counterfeiters overseas. This overseas counterfeiting was usually done in the traditional way of counterfeiters—using the offset printing press.

The offset method of counterfeiting required a knowledge of printing and expensive equipment, such as printing press, high-quality paper, and printing inks. Using the offset process, counterfeiters were able to produce large amounts of counterfeit as opposed to those who used computers who usually printed smaller quantities of notes.

The story I am about to relate to you concerns a traditional counterfeiting operation centered in Helsinki, Finland. You can imagine the dismay of the US Treasury Department when in early 1997, the first counterfeits of the redesigned currency appeared in Eastern Europe and the Baltic states.

This note incorporated many security features, such as the large presidential portrait and the watermark embedded in the paper as genuine US currency. Treasury officials were alarmed. The expensive redesign project was compromised, and the credibility of the US dollar was at stake. Treasury wanted Secret Service to take action, and they wanted the source of these notes to be found.

On May 27, 1997, I received a call from the deputy assistant director for Investigations and the special agent in charge of the Counterfeit Division in Secret Service Headquarters. At the time, I was the assistant to the special agent in charge supervising the criminal squad in the Baltimore field office. I knew both men well, and knowing my investigative and undercover experience, they asked me if I could help them with a counterfeiting case in Helsinki.

They advised me of a confidential source living in the United States who had information on an individual in Helsinki, Finland, who was distributing counterfeit 1996 series one-hundred-dollar bills. The confidential source indicated that this individual was connected to Russian organized crime and that the notes were being printed in Russia.

The confidential source stated that he would be able to arrange a meeting between the individual, Marco, and someone from the United States, and I agreed to be that someone. Because of the urgency of the situation, headquarters wanted me to leave for Finland as soon as possible.

Prior to my departure, I reached out for the confidential source to get a background on Marco and to let him know my cover story. I also contacted the controlling agent of the confidential source to verify the reliability of his information and to determine how trustworthy he was. If I was putting myself in harm's way, I wanted as much information as possible and wanted to make sure the deck wasn't stacked against me.

After I felt comfortable with the situation, I told the confidential source to reach out for Marco and let him know that someone from the US would be coming over to see him. My cover story was that I was an Italian organized crime figure from the States who was interested in buying some high-quality counterfeit currency. Tommy Ferraro was about to go into action.

I departed for Helsinki on the evening of June 2, 1997, on a Finnair flight out of JFK airport in New York City. I arrived in Helsinki the next morning. I was met at the airport by Secret Service agent John James out of our Paris office and two individuals whom I would come to respect and admire during the next several weeks.

Risto and Yergy were members of the Finnish National Bureau of Investigation, or NBI. They were my eyes, ears, and protectors while I was in their country. Risto and Yergy were resourceful and intelligent and were two of the best cops that I had ever worked with during my career. They were very security-conscious and took no chances.

A strange thing happened on my arrival. Marco, the target of the investigation, was at the airport! He walked right past the four of us as I was going to claim my luggage. Yergy broke away from us and followed him to see what he was up to. He watched him attempt to board a flight to Stockholm, Sweden.

Prior to boarding the flight, Marco was stopped by Finnish Customs for having ammunition in his carry-on bag. I also noticed that Marco was on crutches and asked Risto if he knew what happened. Risto advised that word on the street had it that Marco was shot in the leg in a drug deal that went bad!

Great, I was here getting ready to meet a guy who was recently shot in a drug deal gone bad and who was just stopped at the airport with ammunition. My mind began to visualize everything that could go wrong in dealing with a guy like this and how I could minimize my risks. Right then, I knew I would have my work cut out for me but felt up to the challenge.

Upon departing the airport, the four of us went to a café near the Helsinki harbor. It was a beautiful, sunny day, and the water was a picturesque blue. I was enjoying the day and my strong espresso coffee. Yergy and Risto immediately got down to business. They impressed me with their security consciousness.

They were very adamant about not compromising my identity. They advised that all our future meetings would be in clandestine and secluded spots and that I could never be seen at NBI headquarters. I began to feel comfortable with them, and I knew they had my best interest in mind.

The plan was for me to reach out to Marco. The confidential source told him I would be in Helsinki and would be trying to arrange a meeting. The NBI provided me with an undercover mobile phone for that purpose. We drove around the city looking for possible meeting locations and so I could get a feel for the city. We drove to the InterContinental Hotel, the train station, and a shopping mall. I began to familiarize myself with my surroundings. I began to feel the excitement of my situation and could not wait for the action to begin.

The following day, I called Marco using the undercover phone provided by NBI and made contact.

"Hello, Marco."

"Yes?"

"This is Tommy from New York, a friend of Ivan."

"Ah, yes, yes, he told me you may come."

He asked how my flight was, and we exchanged some pleasantries, and then we got down to business. I told him I represented a group from New York that would like to do business with him. I told him I was interested in the product that Ivan told me about. He said that should not be a problem and suggested a meeting.

He asked me where I was staying, and I told him I would let him know once we met. I didn't want him to know where I was staying to prevent surveillance by his associates. He told me that he was in the city of Tampere and asked if I could meet him there. I said to myself, "Where the hell is Tampere?" But I agreed to meet him there.

I told him I would call him and let him know when and where we could meet. I wanted a very public place for our first meeting, and the NBI suggested the Rosenthal Hotel. It would also be an easy place for my protectors at NBI to conduct surveillance.

Tampere, Finland, was a small city about two hours north of Helsinki. I drove there with Yergy and Risto to familiarize myself with Rosenthal Hotel and various other locations throughout the city. NBI had Marco under surveillance at this time and advised that he was in the area. Wouldn't it have been a coincidence if we had run into him again?

NBI was again concerned about surveillance from the undercover meet by Marco's associates. It was decided that I would arrive and depart Rosenthal Hotel by taxi and that on my departure, I would take the taxi to the Tampere train station, walk from the train station to another hotel, and then take a taxi from that hotel to a shopping center.

NBI would be surveilling me that whole time, and if I was not followed, I would be met in a vehicle by NBI agent Kemo and would be taken from the area. As the NBI agents and I were walking through the Rosenthal Hotel, we walked past two of the leaders of organized crime in Finland. These were Marco's bosses. Another strange coincidence! My heart began to race in anticipation of the upcoming meeting. I was in a foreign country on an undercover mission, and I was excited. I was on top of the world.

On June 5, 1997, I placed a call to Marco saying that I was on my way to Tampere and that I would call him in an hour and a half to let him know where I would be. He asked if I was coming alone, and I didn't answer him one way or another. I didn't want him to know too much for safety concerns.

Just as I began thinking about my safety during the meeting, Risto came to me and handed me a Smith & Wesson Model 60 .38 revolver, which was his personal weapon. He said, "I think you should take this, but this is between you and me. If my bosses find out about this, I would lose my job."

He expressed to me his concern for my safety and thought I should have it with me. I agreed and took the weapon and placed it in my belt under my shirt. I began to think about what an honorable man Risto was and how he put himself at risk out of concern for my safety. I felt very secure with my NBI protectors.

The weather in Finland was exceptionally warm this June, and I was glad to leave my hotel room at Scandic Pasila. The hotel was a small one located in a residential area away from downtown Helsinki. This was done to limit the possibility of me running into Marco or one of his associates downtown. The room had no air-conditioning, and this warm weather made it stifling.

It was a very pleasant ride to Tampere on this beautiful, sunny day, and I enjoyed the sights of the Finnish countryside, and I was sure glad to get out of that hotel room. After an hour and a half into our trip, Risto pulled over the car in a small town, and I made a phone call to Marco.

I told him I would be in Tampere at 1:30 p.m., and he suggested that we meet at Hotel Ileves. He suggested this because this hotel was frequented by local organized crime figures. NBI had previously briefed me regarding this issue, and I suggested that we meet at the Rosenthal Hotel, and Marco agreed. He suggested that we could meet there and take a ride in his car. I had no intention of leaving in Marco's car and told him so right away. Marco said that he understood, and we agreed to meet at the restaurant in the hotel.

The NBI preparation for this meeting was exceptional and made me feel very comfortable in my undercover role. A pen register was set up on Marco's phone to capture what telephone numbers were being called and received. Two hotel rooms were rented by NBI that covered all access roads to the hotel in order to observe any known associates of Marco entering the hotel.

Risto and a female NBI agent would be at a table in the restaurant in close proximity, and an NBI agent who looked like a Euro hippie with a ponytail, backpack, and Birkenstock sandals would be at the train station to follow me back to Helsinki should I have to depart Tampere via train.

The plan was developed that I would meet Marco, purchase the counterfeit currency, and depart separately. I would leave the hotel via taxi and go to the Tampere train station. NBI would observe me going to the station to determine if I was being followed. Once at the train station, I would call Risto and be directed to a department store via taxi. Once at the department store, I would be directed to a store exit where I would be picked up by the NBI.

I arrived at the hotel and took a table in the restaurant. My NBI covering teams were already there in the restaurant and hotel lobby. Marco arrived about twenty minutes later on his crutches. He was in his midthirties, about six foot three, and weighed 230 pounds. He had a scraggly beard and a rough look, like he was partying the night before.

The restaurant was not crowded, and he came right to my table. "Marco, please have a seat," I said. He apologized for being late, and we exchanged pleasantries. I offered him a drink, but he declined the offer because he was driving. *Wow, what a law-abiding drug dealer,* I thought. I think the real reason he didn't want a drink was because he was hungover.

It was a cordial meeting, and we spoke very freely. I gave him the impression that I was an Italian organized figure from New York, and he spoke about his criminal activity in Finland. I told him I was very interested in the new note (redesigned 1996 series US currency) that Ivan said he had access to. He said that he only had a sample of the new note and that it was still being printed. I said a sample would be fine but that I was interested in a large quantity.

"Tommy, let me ask you. With all your connections in New York, why do you need me to provide you with counterfeit currency?" he asked.

I anticipated this question and had an answer ready for him. I told him that through my connections in Las Vegas casinos, I planned to switch the counterfeit currency for genuine currency in the casino cash rooms. I told him that by having the counterfeit printed overseas, it would be difficult for authorities to trace its origin. If the counterfeit was produced in the US, there would be too many people involved who could implicate me. Printing overseas would minimize my risk.

I told him that my organization had the resources to have the money transported back to the US once we concluded our transaction. He seemed to buy my story. I again asked about the new note, and Marco became evasive, saying it was still being printed. I dropped the questions about the new note, and we ordered lunch.

We enjoyed a nice filet mignon compliments of my NBI counterparts, and then I got back to business. Marco said he would not be able to get me a large quantity of the new note but said that he might be able to get me a quantity of the older note. My mission was to buy the new 1996 series counterfeit notes; however, to keep the case moving, I was willing to buy any counterfeit that he could provide.

I got right to the point and told him I wanted to buy $10,000 today with a sample of the new note to show my associates. I stated that I would pay him $2,000, or 20 percent, for the counterfeit. Marco agreed to get the package but said, "I hope you are not a cop."

"You don't think I'm a cop, or you wouldn't be here speaking to me. You look like you are smarter than that," I said.

Marco paused for a moment and then brought up the informant. "I told Ivan that the price was 30 percent," he said. That was not the price I discussed with the informant, so I knew Marco was already trying to rip me off, but I agreed to the 30 percent to keep the case moving.

I told him I wanted a better price once we did the bigger deal. Marco stated that he would be back in an hour and asked if I could meet him at the back bar. I had not seen the back bar but agreed to meet him there. I felt the NBI would be able to cover the deal. Upon his departure, Marco was surveilled by NBI and observed going to several locations in Tampere. His movement provided good intelligence for possible locations of the counterfeit currency; however, NBI lost him during the surveillance and could not locate him.

An hour passed, and Marco did not return. An hour and a half and still a no-show. Maybe I scared him off. Maybe he felt that I was a cop. Finally, about two hours later, Marco returned. He came to the bar as agreed, but he did not have the package with him.

"Come with me to my Mercedes. I have your package in the car," he said.

"I'm not going anywhere. Bring the package here," I said.

Marco told me he didn't like to handle the package because his fingerprints would be on it, but he agreed to go get it. He stated, "I hope this is not a bust."

I replied, "I hope it is not either, but I have good lawyers."

We both had a laugh, and he told me that he was almost forty and that he had never been arrested. I stated that I had never been arrested either. He replied that I was in a much higher position than him, which protected me from arrest. With that comment, I felt that I really sold myself as a New York wise guy to Marco. I knew I had him hooked.

Marco returned to the bar about five minutes later and handed me a yellow plastic pouch with Forex Currency Exchange printed on the outside. I held it below the bar in front of me and opened it out of view of those people in the bar area. Inside was a stack of counterfeit hundred-dollar bills, which appeared to be the $10,000 we had agreed upon.

As expected, it was not the new note or 1996 series US currency but an older note. I then handed Marco an envelope with $3,000 in genuine US currency. When I handed Marco the envelope, he had this scared look on his face like he was about to get pounced on by twenty cops. I told him to relax and that everything was good. I said that he should leave before me and that I would contact him in a few days.

Marco quickly left through a side door of the bar, and when he got to his car, he probably exhaled a sigh of relief that he was not arrested. I waited about five minutes and departed the hotel by taxi. I called my NBI counterparts and told them I was on the way to the Tampere railway station. Upon arrival at the station, I had my previously noted encounter with the police officer.

I sat in the restroom of the railway station hoping that there would be no knock on the stall door. My heart was pounding. If this police officer stopped me for questioning and patted me down, he was going to find the counterfeit currency and the gun. With Europe's provocation rules concerning investigations, law enforcement officers were not permitted to commit criminal acts while working in an undercover capacity.

If the officer found the contraband, I would be arrested and would have no defense that I was working undercover with the NBI. It would create an issue for Secret Service and the State Department, and I could wind up in a Finnish prison.

I sat there for what seemed like an eternity, but there was no knock. I slowly opened the door and looked around the restroom. No police officers! I made my way out of the train station through a side door and hopped into a taxi. I had just dodged a bullet. I was very lucky that police officer did not investigate further.

As instructed by the NBI and after some language difficulties, I told the taxi driver to take me to Sokos department store. NBI had me under surveillance to make sure I was not being followed. I entered the department store by a side door, and after about ten minutes of browsing in the men's department, Risto called me and told me to exit the side door opposite from where I entered.

As I exited, Kemo was there just as planned, and I jumped in his vehicle. We took a back way out of Tampere, and about five miles out of town, we met up with Yergy and SA James. I jumped in their vehicle, and we headed south to Helsinki.

We drove to an outdoor café overlooking the Baltic Sea. It was a beautiful June day, and we ordered some beer and debriefed the operation. We felt good about how the deal went; however, we needed to set up another deal for the new note, which was the primary mission of this investigation.

To avoid accidental contact with Marco or one of his associates, the NBI suggested that I leave Helsinki for the weekend. Since Helsinki was having a heat wave and my hotel was hot as hell, that sounded like a great idea to me. SA James asked me where I wanted to go, and I told him Paris. It was decided that I would leave Helsinki the next day, which was a Friday, travel to Paris, and return to Helsinki on Monday, June 10. I would make contact with Marco on Tuesday to set up our next meeting.

I departed for Paris on June 7, 1997. I was supposed to leave the previous day, and to the dismay of the NBI, I did not. The flight was too early, and I was physically drained and decided to leave the next day. The NBI was very anxious to get me out of town and was relieved when I was on my way to Paris.

I boarded an Air France flight and traveled business class for the three-hour flight. Upon arrival, I took a taxi to Royal Hotel, a quaint hotel near the Arc de Triomphe and Champs-Élysées. Royal Hotel was the perfect place to stay while I was lying low prior to the next undercover deal. I felt like James Bond on the loose in Europe!

At the hotel, I ran into a friend from Secret Service who was in town with his wife, and the three of us had a great dinner at a French restaurant that evening. The following day, I did a walking tour of Paris by myself. Paris was a very beautiful city and very easy to walk around. Follow the river Seine and you could find most points of interest.

I walked from the hotel to the Arc de Triomphe and from the Arc de Triomphe to the Eiffel Tower and from the Eiffel Tower to the Notre-Dame. At the cathedral, I attended a prayer service, which was beautiful in the French language. I then headed down to the Champs-Élysées to the Louvre but did not go in and then back to the hotel.

During the walk, I stopped at several outside coffeehouses for café le crème or a beer. I really enjoyed sitting there, taking in the sights and sounds of Paris. It was a relaxing walk on a beautiful day, one that I will never forget. I walked about twelve miles that day and enjoyed every minute of it.

The next day, I stopped by the Secret Service field office which is located at the US Embassy to pick up my tickets for the return flight to Helsinki. I had a great couple of days, but knew I would have to get back into Tommy Ferraro mode once I got back to Helsinki. With the undercover cell phone provided by the NBI, I reached out to Marco in Finland.

I told him that my associates in the US were very interested in the new note and that I wanted to take $5,000,000 for delivery next week in Helsinki. Marco stated that he could arrange this, but that he must contact someone from outside the country. He stated that the product was not in Finland. I told Marco that I would call him at the same time tomorrow to see what the guy from out of the country had to say.

I really wanted to see the *Mona Lisa*, and because the Louvre was closed the previous day when I walked by, I decided to go back. I left the hotel, walked about four miles to the Louvre, and viewed one of the most famous paintings in the world. It was a long walk but very much worth it. It was not every day one got to Paris, so I made the most of my time there.

On June 10, 1997, I traveled back to Helsinki via Air France business class and took a taxi back to the Scandic Pasila. It was a very hot day. The hotel had no air-conditioning, and my room was stifling. I was glad to get out of the room and meet with John, Yergy, Risto, and Kemo.

We drove around the city looking for possible locations for my next meeting with Marco. We went to Market Square, the railway station, and Postibank. A plan was developed that I would meet Marco at Market Square, take him to Postibank, and flash him $500,000 in genuine currency, then meet him at the railway station for the exchange of the genuine for the counterfeit.

The railway station was picked because it would be easy for the NBI to cover the deal there. It was decided that I would rent a safe deposit box at Postibank and store the $500,000 there. I would bring Marco to the bank and flash him the $500,000 in the safe deposit box vault area. Again, the bank was picked because the NBI could cover the vault easily and surveil me in the vault area by video just in case Marco planned to rip me off.

I had one problem. In order to rent a safe deposit box, I would have to produce a passport. Obviously, working undercover, I could not use my US government passport, and I did not have an undercover passport. Due to Europe's agent provocateur laws, the NBI could not help me rent the safe deposit box. I was on my own for this phase of the operation, so I came up with a plan.

I decided to walk in, produce my undercover Maryland driver's license, give the bank manager a story, and attempt to rent the safe deposit box. It worked. I told the manager that I lost my passport and was waiting for a replacement and that I needed to store some valuables while I was in Helsinki. I was convincing, and he rented me the box.

The plan was coming together. Now all I needed was $500,000 in US currency. SA James had already made contact with Secret Service Headquarters counterfeit division, and DAD Steve Mattone and SAIC Dennis Lyons were en route to Helsinki on a commercial flight with a briefcase stuffed with $500,000.

Upon their arrival, I met them on the street near the Postibank, and covered very closely by the NBI, they handed me a large satchel with $500,000 in genuine US currency. Mattone, Lyons, and I were good friends having worked together at the Baltimore field office and were the individuals who decided that I should do the undercover on this case.

As they handed me the briefcase, I gave them a wink and said that I would see them in South America. We all got a laugh, and I proceeded into the bank to secure the cash in my safe deposit box. With the cash secured, I reached out for Marco.

I walked to the railway station, which was a short distance from the bank, and placed the call. Marco advised that he met with his contact from out of the country today. He stated that his contact was interested in doing a deal and that he would have more information tomorrow. He stated that his contact might want to do a small deal first and that his contact was wondering how I could put such a large deal together.

This question got my attention. Was he asking that because he didn't trust me, or was he asking because he didn't think I could come up with the cash? I felt that it was probably a little of both. I told him not to worry about me but concentrate on getting more definitive information from his contact. I told him I would call him the following day and that, hopefully, he would have more information for me.

I called Marco the following day; however, he could still not give me any more information about his contact providing the new 1996 notes. I began to doubt whether Marco had a contact and if he was going to be able to set up the deal. I wondered if he was nervous, or was he trying to set me up for a rip-off?

Could he produce the new note, or was he just talking? He did provide me a package of counterfeit already, so I knew he had access to counterfeit. I decided that another face-to-face meeting would be the best way to proceed and set up a meeting for the following day near the town square.

Prior to the meet, it was decided that I would do a surprise flash of the $500,000 at the bank. If Marco or his associate had any concerns about me being able to complete my end of the deal, this should ease those concerns. However, once he saw the cash, it could also set in motion a plan to rip me off. Either way, we could cover it, so we decided to go this route to keep the case moving. I called Marco and set up the meeting for the following day.

On June 12, 1997, I met Marco in the town square near the cruise ship terminal. I picked this spot because it was a very busy area and would allow my NBI counterparts to cover the meeting without any problems. The NBI was very concerned about me being followed by Marco's associates or countersurveillance during the meet, so I left the hotel by myself, boarded the no. 7 tram, and got off by Stockmann's department store.

The NBI was already in place to observe me exit the tram and determine if I was being followed. I walked for about five blocks and met Marco at a statue in the town square. We walked to a café nearby and had coffee. Marco told me he did not have a definitive answer on the deal to purchase the new note. He stated that his contact and the money was in Estonia, a country across the Baltic Sea from Finland and formerly part of the Soviet Union.

He said that there was a good market for the counterfeit in Russia and that maybe his associate wanted to sell it there. This was the first time he told me where the money was, so I felt like I was making some progress, if he was not bullshitting me and setting me up for a rip-off. I told him to take a walk with me, and we walked several blocks to the Postibank.

The NBI was already set up in the bank, ready to observe me the whole time on the bank's video camera system. We entered the bank, and I told Marco to wait downstairs. I went upstairs to the vault area and produced my Tommy Ferraro ID to the vault attendant. I wanted to make sure no one else was there, and after determining that it was clear, I walked halfway down the stairs and motioned for Marco to come up.

He had this puzzled look and was probably wondering what I was doing. I put him in a small room that bank customers used for privacy when opening their safe deposit boxes and went to my safe deposit box. I returned to the room with $500,000. I placed it on the table and separated it into five bricks of $100,000 each.

Marco's eyes opened wide as he looked at the cash. I told him it was all genuine US currency, and he said I didn't have to take it apart since he believed me. For effect, I pulled out a pack of $10,000 and handed it to him. He began to feel it and look at it and gave me a big smile. I told him, "Now you know what I can do. Let's see what you can do."

I took the pack from him, placed it in the container with the rest of the money, and told Marco to wait in the room. I left the room, returned to the vault, and attempted to secure the cash in box no. 1238, but I had a problem. The lock was stuck and would not open! I tried several times but no luck. I sensed that the NBI counterparts who were observing me were nervous.

I tried the second key, but it still would not open. Finally, after numerous tries, it opened! I put the cash in, locked the door, and breathed a sigh of relief. We departed the bank, and Marco immediately began to make phone calls. By his reaction to the cash, I felt that I had him hooked!

We went back to the same café to talk business. Marco began to provide more details about his contacts. He told me that an associate in Helsinki had the contact in Tallinn, Estonia, with the individuals who had the new note. He also told me he had $2,000,000 of the note that I previously purchased from him in Helsinki.

Again, I stressed to him that I was interested in the new note and was ready to do business. I reminded him that I just showed him $500,000 and was ready to buy. Now it was up to him to put the deal together. Marco then asked me if I was interested in buying machine guns or drugs. I told him to slow down.

"Let's do this deal first. If everything goes well, we have plenty of opportunities for more business, but let's not get ahead of ourselves." He agreed and said that he was going to take the ferry to Estonia to meet with his associate and the Estonians.

I told Marco that I would call him later to see if he had any further information. Prior to his departure for the ferry, I noticed a handgun in Marco's fanny pack. I couldn't believe it! I just flashed this guy half a million dollars, and he was armed. I made two mistakes. I should have checked him for guns before the flash, and I should have made a point to borrow Risto's gun again. Live and learn.

The sight of that gun made me even more cautious of a rip-off. I called Risto, told him about the firearm, and asked that he bring his .38 when we meet. I picked up the gun later that day and always had it with me for the rest of my time in Finland.

I spoke to Marco the next day upon his return from Estonia. He told me he was unable to get samples of the new note. He said that he had met the Estonians and that they were very cautious. He said that they wanted to do a smaller $100,000 deal and that they wanted me to come to Estonia. Additionally, they wanted me to front the money!

"Are you kidding me?" I exclaimed. "Do they think I'm an idiot? No way I'm traveling to Estonia, and I never front any money. That's not the way I do business." For my safety, I could never travel to Estonia, and fronting the money was just inviting a rip-off. I had to push to do the deal in Helsinki.

"As I told you, you know what I can do. I have the cash. Let them know that, and tell them that I will only do the deal in Finland, and I will not front any money." Marco said he would call me later once he spoke to them. I began to get an uneasy feeling. Either the Estonians put ideas in Marco's head that I might be a cop, or he was setting me up for a rip-off.

Marco called me later that day and stated that the Estonians were very cautious and were worried that the counterfeit might get intercepted in transit. They were pushing for me to come to Estonia. "I guess we are at an impasse," I said. "I don't do business that way. It's up to you to convince them if this deal is going to happen."

Marco called again and asked if I would be interested in the old note that I previously purchased. I told him that my people were more interested in the new note and to keep trying to set up the deal. Marco called again and said he still had no luck with the Estonians.

Finally, on the fourth phone call, Marco told me that the Estonians had agreed to let him do the deal in Helsinki and that he was arranging for the money to be brought by boat to Helsinki. He said that $5,000,000 would be sent. "Wonderful," I said. "Call me when it's here."

Marco called me again later that day. He wanted to meet me that night. He said the money was in Helsinki. Since he knew that I had $500,000, the call got me thinking about a setup for a kidnapping or a rip-off, so I declined to meet him and told him I would see him the following day.

My NBI counterparts had gone home for the day, so there was no way I could be covered if we met. Later that evening, I met with Agents James, Mattone, and Lyons at their hotel and briefed them as to what transpired that day. They advised me that they were briefed by the NBI and that they were very concerned for my safety.

The NBI told them that four of Marco's criminal associates had arrived in town, including the boss of the organization. Mattone suggested that when the meet occurs, he, Jordan, and Lyons would cover it with the NBI. That was fine with me. The more Secret Service agents, the better!

Although they were not permitted to carry firearms while in the country, Mattone explained to us that he was going to bring a gun and shoot somebody if necessary. James got a very worried look on his face at this comment since he was the permanent representative of Secret Service in Finland until he realized that Mattone was only kidding about bringing a gun. That was the type of guy Mattone was, always a jokester.

I left the meeting, hopped in a cab, and returned to my stifling hotel room. I lay on the bed and thought about tomorrow's impending deal and had Risto's revolver right next to me on the nightstand.

I woke up on the morning of June 13, 1997, and began to prepare myself for the meeting. It was Friday the Thirteenth, and I thought that this was going to be an unlucky day for somebody, hopefully not me.

A plan was developed by the NBI and Secret Service to tell Marco that my $500,000 would be at the railway station and to have him bring the $5,000,000. Once at the station, I would tell him that I needed to see the counterfeit before we could go any further. If he was for real, he should have no problem showing me the counterfeit since I had already flashed him $500,000.

My $500,000 would be nowhere near the station and was already secured by Mattone and Lynch for transport back to Washington. Once I viewed the counterfeit, I would tell Marco that I would call him in a few minutes to tell him where we could do the exchange. Once I departed from Marco, I would call the NBI and let them know that the counterfeit was there, and they would move in for the arrest.

As I explained, because of Europe's agent provocateur rules, I could not be part of the deal. I would have to walk away, blend into the crowd, and be the guy who got away. If all went well, Marco would be in cuffs, and I would be on a plane on the way back to the United States.

NBI was very meticulous in the preparation for the meet and assigned fifteen agents to cover me. Additionally, Secret Service agents Mattone, Lyons, and James would be covering me. For my safety, I would be under constant surveillance, and NBI stressed that there should be no deviation from that plan. The plan was simple enough; however, deals like this never went smoothly.

I called Marco that morning and set up a meeting for 1:00 p.m. near the main entrance of the station. I picked this location because it would be easy for the NBI surveillance teams to blend in with the crowd. I told Marco that my money would be at the station and to come prepared to do the deal.

As soon as I told Marco that I wanted to see the counterfeit, he became very evasive. He said he didn't want to be near the counterfeit when the deal was done and then said he wanted to do a smaller deal of about $600,000. He stated that he had two other guys who would do the deal with me.

His reaction got my attention, and I did not get a very good feeling about this deal. I felt like I was being set up for a rip-off since they knew I was sitting on $500,000 in genuine currency. Despite this feeling, I met Marco at the train station, very closely covered by the NBI.

I had a very animated conversation with him laced with expletives to let him know I was very upset. I told him that I had shown him $500,000 and that now it was his time to put up or shut up. I told him that before we went any further, I needed to see the counterfeit. He responded by saying that he would have to talk to his associates one more time.

His response made me cautious, but I kept pressing him. To get things moving, I showed him a locker key to one of the lockers at the train station and told him that the $500,000 was at the train station. I told him to meet me back there in twenty minutes and that the deal had to be done today because I was going back to the United States today.

The part about me going to the United States was true. It was decided that if the deal could not be completed today, it was probably going to be a rip-off; and for my safety, I should leave Finland immediately. I already had my plane tickets and was checked in for a flight that evening.

Marco left and agreed to meet me at the same location in twenty minutes after he talked to his associates. As he left, the realization of what I had just done set in. I showed him a locker key, and now he thought the $500,000 was at the train station. If this was going to be a rip-off, Marco and his associates had every reason to do it now.

I immediately left the front of the train station, went inside, and called the NBI to apprise them of the situation and to make sure there were close covering agents. I then went to the restroom, removed the .38 revolver from my pocket, and placed it in my waistband, covered by my shirt. If there was going to be trouble today, I wanted easy access to it.

NBI advised me that they observed about a dozen of Marco's associates in and around the train station and felt that based on this number and Marco's actions, I was being set up for a rip-off. I agreed and said we should probably call off the deal. Marco returned to my location in about twenty minutes and was still stalling about showing me the counterfeit. I gave him an expletive-laced outburst of what I thought of him and walked away. The deal was over.

I was covered very closely by the NBI in case any of Marco's associates were following me, and I hopped in a taxi. I had the driver take me toward my hotel, and when I received a call from the NBI that all was clear, I told the driver to pull over, and I jumped into an NBI vehicle with Risto and Yergy and was on my way to the airport.

I went through customs immediately and boarded the plane. Risto and Yergy stood on the Jetway until the door was locked to ensure that none of Marco's associates boarded the plane. The plane lifted off, and I breathed a sigh of relief that I was out of the country.

That evening, I was back on United States soil. Two days later, I was in New York City on a protective assignment as the detail leader for the visit of the prime minister of Romania to the United States. Such was the life of a Secret Service agent. One day, I was in Europe working undercover with counterfeiters; and the next day, I was a representative of the United States government, dealing with a foreign head of government.

The story of Marco did not end there. He was involved in drug dealing, arms trafficking, and counterfeiting and was eventually

arrested by the NBI on drug charges. During a search of his residence, agents uncovered drugs and counterfeit currency. The counterfeit seized was the same type of note as the $10,000 package I
purchased from him.

He was charged with the drugs and counterfeit and spent time
in a Finnish jail. The new note was not found during the search,
and Marco did not cooperate with the investigation. Based upon the
outcome, I believe we made a good call in calling off my deal with
Marco. He most likely did not have the new note and was setting me
up for a rip-off of the $500,000. At least he spent time in jail and
justice was served.

SUPER NOTE

I n 1996, Secret Service was in the middle of one of the most challenging criminal investigations in its history. The case centered on a high-quality counterfeit one-hundred-dollar bill, nearly undetectable to the untrained eye, that was flooding the world market. This super note was being produced in Asia and had become such a significant problem that the US Treasury totally redesigned the one-hundred-dollar bill to make it much harder to counterfeit.

Under this backdrop, Secret Service set up a task force in Bangkok, Thailand, to work with Thai and other East Asian authorities in an attempt to suppress this counterfeiting operation. I was selected as a member of the task force and spent thirty days in Bangkok on the trail of the counterfeiters.

In the previous cases that I recounted, I was usually working in an undercover capacity, buying or selling contraband. For this assignment, I did not work undercover. I was a member of the team following up on leads, conducting interviews, and traveling to several other countries to meet with foreign authorities. It was a very interesting case in which I got to see the inner workings of foreign law enforcement authorities and foreign judicial systems.

On the evening of February 13, 1996, I departed Washington, DC, for Bangkok, Thailand. I caught a connecting flight in London and settled in for the seven-thousand-mile flight to Bangkok. The flight would be twelve hours and travel over Eastern Europe—

Istanbul, Turkey; Tehran, Iran; Karachi, Pakistan; Kolkata, India; Rangoon, Burma; and then into Bangkok. Thankfully, I was authorized to fly business class, which made it a very pleasant flight.

I arrived in Bangkok the following morning and was met by a member of the task force. I was driven to the Grand Hyatt Erawan, my home for the next thirty days. The Erawan was an outstanding five-star hotel that made my stay very comfortable.

Bangkok was a very crowded city and was called the Venice of the East with its rivers and many canals. The pollution was horrendous, and there were hundreds of motorcycles dodging in and out of traffic. It was a really tough place to get around, which would add another factor to our investigation.

The following day, we had a task force meeting at the hotel, and I and several other new members were briefed on the work of the task force thus far. We learned that there were teams working in Phnom Penh, Cambodia, and Kuala Lumpur, Malaysia, and that we would be traveling to other countries also. We were provided briefings on each of the suspects and which countries they were operating from.

About two days later, we had our first field operation. At 5:00 a.m., SA Jim Galler and I met members of the Thai Office of the Narcotics Control Board (ONCD) and the Royal Thai Police for what we thought was the execution of an arrest warrant against counterfeiting suspect Loppachi, who had been identified as passing several counterfeit notes in Bangkok.

We were familiar with Loppachi from our briefing several days ago. Jim and I did not speak Thai, and the officers spoke very little English, so there was miscommunication from the beginning. The suspect's house was about an hour's drive from the hotel. The house was located on a small, narrow backstreet, and it was still dark when we arrived at the residence. There were stray dogs sleeping all over the street, but the neighborhood was fairly decent with some gated homes.

At the residence, a Thai police officer got out of the car in the dark and rang the bell. There was no surveillance, no ruse calls, and I thought this was an odd way to effect an arrest warrant. That was when we realized we didn't have an arrest warrant! The Thai police were going to ask the suspect if he would talk to us. It went from an arrest warrant to a "Please talk to me" request.

I was not feeling good about the situation. We were in a dark backstreet in Bangkok, stray dogs all around, and the suspect's dog was barking wildly at us. Jim and I were unarmed, we were not sure if the Thai police were armed, and the language difficulties did not help the situation.

The Thai police officer rang the bell numerous times, but there was no answer. We decided to come back to the residence a little later. I found a phone booth in the middle of nowhere and made a call to the task force to advise them of the situation. We tried a second time; however, there was no answer again. We decided to get a cup of coffee and return later.

The Thai officers took us to a local 7-Eleven store, which was surprisingly just like a 7-Eleven in the United States. On the third trip to the residence, the suspect finally answered the door. The suspect invited us in and agreed to talk to us. We requested that he accompany us to a downtown hotel for an interview, and he agreed. He only requested that he be permitted to take a shower prior to leaving. We permitted him to take a shower, but I watched him as closely as I could, while still giving him privacy. All I could picture was him emerging from the back room with an AK-47, shooting up the place!

We departed the residence without incident and headed downtown to the Imperial Hotel. We decided upon the Imperial because it was far away from our hotel location. We drove with a Thai police in the suspect's car to that hotel. In the United States, we would never drive in the suspect's car, but we were in Thailand. Things were done differently there!

During the interview, Loppachi was somewhat cooperative but evasive and not completely truthful. It was very interesting interviewing someone from a different culture. It was totally different from dealing with wise guys from Brooklyn!

Loppachi admitted to being a dealer of counterfeit cigarettes but claimed no knowledge of counterfeit currency. In Southeast Asia, counterfeit cigarettes was a big business. The counterfeiters would use inferior tobacco and create packaging to make the cigarettes appear to be American manufactured brands, such as Marlboro and Newport. When confronted with the evidence against him in passing several counterfeit notes, Loppachi claimed he didn't know that the notes were counterfeit and stated that he received them in a transaction of selling counterfeit cigarettes.

We concluded our meeting and directed Loppachi to return to the hotel the following morning. The following day, Loppachi returned, and we continued our interview. Loppachi was very evasive, and all of a sudden, language became a problem. The Thai police helped with interpretation; however, the interview went nowhere.

Loppachi did agree to take a polygraph, which was scheduled for the next day. Loppachi was deceptive during the polygraph and made some more admissions about his dealing in counterfeit cigarettes; however, he still claimed no knowledge of the counterfeit currency.

He did, however, state that the counterfeit currency probably came from Kuala Lumpur, Malaysia, where his contacts for the counterfeit cigarettes conducted business. His admission of the Kuala Lumpur connection was in line with intelligence the task force received regarding Kuala Lumpur, which corroborated his information somewhat. Now we had a new direction to go in.

The following day, we executed a search warrant at the residence of an individual named Ronnie Tan. Information was developed that Tan was a distributor of the counterfeit currency. The warrant should have been executed a week earlier but was met with some resistance from someone within the Royal Thai Police.

A colonel from the Thai military and an inspector from the Royal Thai Police were present during the execution of the warrant. Upon arrival, we found several individuals in the house; however, Tan was not there. Most of Tan's belongings were gone, and what remained were about to be taken from the house by one of the individuals.

The individuals were very cooperative, and we searched the remainder of Tan's belongings and the rest of the house but uncovered nothing of investigative value. The individual who was taking

Tan's belongings from the residence agreed, after some persuasion from the colonel, to let us search his residence and office.

The individual, Niyom Parsat, was a character. He was animated and somewhat goofy and lived in a large house with his mother-in-law. His house was in a province about an hour and a half from Bangkok, and to get there, we drove in the absolute worst traffic I had ever seen.

During the search, we found numerous items of investigative value. Items seized included photos, credit card accounts, bank records, and passports. It was amazing to me how easily we were able to conduct search warrants in a foreign country as guests of the local authorities. Too bad there was a week's delay in getting this warrant. It gave time for Tan to relocate. It made me wonder if we had a leak inside the Royal Thai Police that warned him and delayed the warrant.

After several days of interviews and search warrants, we were ready for a little rest and relaxation. Several of the task force members took a *tuk tuk*, which was a three-wheeled motorcycle, to get fitted for custom suits. Jesse's, a suit maker on Sukhumvit Road, was a well-known establishment and recommended by the US Embassy. The traffic in this city was horrendous, in my opinion the worst in the world. Motorcycles were everywhere, and there were no rules on the road. It was a dangerous trip to the suit maker!

On February 25, 1996, we got back to work and conducted two additional search warrants at a residence and a business with the Royal Thai Police. It was very easy to get a search warrant in Thailand. Prior to going to the residence, we went to the local police district, and the Thai officers explained the situation to a local colonel and completed some paperwork. Just like that, the warrant was issued.

At the residence, an eighty-year-old man, when confronted by the Thai police, ran and climbed a wall into his neighbor's backyard. This was a pretty bizarre scene, and I began to compare this situation with Thai officers trying to execute search warrants in New York City. In reality, it would never happen, yet we were in Thailand, fully assisting in the execution of the warrants. We had it very easy there. The police were very liberal and allowed us to search without restriction.

During the search, I didn't find any counterfeit US currency; however, I found a drawer full of Thai currency in the old man's desk. The man's son showed up at the residence and became very upset with the police, who quickly put him in his place. We left the residence without incident and without any other investigative leads.

The following day, several task force members took a break from the investigation and did some sightseeing. As I previously stated, Bangkok is called the Venice of the East with its many rivers and canals. We took a boat ride on the river to the floating market. The river was very dirty with many small shacks built along the canals.

As we rode along, many small boats approached our boat to sell us items. The floating market was a collection of souvenir shops along the riverbank. We proceeded from there by boat to the Thonburi Snake Farm. We saw an awesome show where snake handlers performed with poisonous cobra and other snakes. We actually got there early and took seats in the front row and saw up close the handler milking the venom from a cobra's fangs.

As the crowd began to close in behind us, I became worried about the loose snakes in front of us. The show was done without any barriers between the snakes and the crowd, and with one mistake, I could have had a cobra in my lap! With the large crowd behind us, there was no place to go. Thankfully, we left the show without any snakebite.

The snake farm was an amazing place with its collection of tigers, snakes, and other exotic animals. On the way out, I took an amazing picture with a twelve-foot python wrapped around my neck. From there, the group proceeded to the Samphran Elephant Ground and Zoo north of Bangkok. This was another amazing place.

They had two large tigers, uncaged tigers that were chained down. I was able to sit down behind them, hold both of their tails, and take a photo. It was an amazing photo, but I was sure the tigers were sedated to prevent them from tearing my head off!

We also saw a crocodile show where the handlers put their faces in the mouths of the crocodiles. It was an amazing and scary show!

We also saw an elephant show, and I took a ride on an elephant. It was a pretty good day interacting with exotic wildlife for a kid from Brooklyn!

On February 27, 1996, I made a telephone call to the Economic Crimes branch of the Singapore Police Force. I had received an assignment to interview Eric Schofield, a resident of Singapore and associate of Ronnie Tan and Loppachi. The call was a request for assistance in locating Schofield and facilitating an interview. I received a callback later that afternoon and was advised that Economic Crimes had set up a meeting with Schofield for the next day at 10:00 a.m. It was amazing how cooperative people were with the Singapore police!

Another task force member and I took a Thai Airways flight to Singapore the next morning. It was a two-and-a-half-hour flight, and the plane was filled to capacity. Of course, I had a middle seat. It took forever to clear Singapore Customs and to get a taxi, but we finally made it to the Carlton Hotel. I was impressed at how very clean and orderly the city of Singapore was, a sharp contrast to Bangkok.

The following day, we met the resident security officer (RSO) at the US Embassy. Whenever conducting official business overseas, the embassy should be aware of your activities. The RSO said he was not aware that we were coming but quickly agreed to assist us in any way. We took a taxi to the Singapore Police Criminal Investigation Department and met with the assistant superintendent of police and Schofield.

By the presence of the superintendent, I knew that Schofield must have had some political connections in Singapore and was not hopeful of gaining anything from the interview. The interview of Schofield was very cordial, but I felt he was being untruthful when we asked him if he knew where we could locate Ronnie Tan. He advised that if he located Tan, he would try to arrange his surrender via the Singapore police. I preferred that Tan surrender to the Bangkok police to avoid extradition issues, but at this point, we would take whatever we could get.

My partner and I took a walk in downtown Singapore in stifling heat and then took a taxi to the World Trade Center and a ferry to

Sentosa Island. We viewed the remnants of the British fort and the history of the fall of Singapore in World War II.

Prior to our departure to Singapore, we received an assignment to also travel to Kuala Lumpur, Malaysia. We were tasked with briefing the Malaysian authorities on the progress of our counterfeiting investigation. We traveled back to Carlton Hotel, packed our bags into a taxi, and headed to the airport. We arrived in Kuala Lumpur that evening and stayed at the MiCasa All Suite Hotel, a five-star location.

On February 29, 1996, we met with the RSO and other officials at the US Embassy as was the protocol as I previously explained. We gave the embassy officials a briefing on our counterfeit investigation and then went to a prearranged meeting with the Malaysian Special Branch, the intelligence arm of the Malaysian government. We provided them a briefing on our investigation and, in particular, the information we received that the source of the counterfeit notes in Bangkok was from Kuala Lumpur and involved in the counterfeit cigarette trade.

We requested assistance from the Special Branch, and they agreed to help but wanted a formal request in writing. We hinted at the fact that we might have to set up a wiretap if we received further information about counterfeiting activities in Malaysia but would wait until we had a formal cooperation agreement in writing.

Upon the conclusion of the meeting, we traveled back to the US Embassy to brief the deputy chief of mission (DCM), the second-highest official at the embassy. The DCM could ensure that cooperation agreement with Special Branch could be put on the fast track, and we wanted to be sure he was onboard.

That afternoon, I took a walk around downtown Kuala Lumpur. As I walked, I passed hundreds of street vendors with counterfeit Gucci, Rolex, Polo, etc. The city was a counterfeiter's paradise! I began to feel that the task force was looking in the right direction. However, I wondered how much cooperation we would get from the local authorities if the counterfeit items I observed were so much out in the open and ignored. It seemed that counterfeiting was widely accepted in Malaysia.

We had dinner at the Hard Rock Cafe that evening and traveled back to Bangkok the next morning. I felt that our trip to Singapore and Malaysia was somewhat productive as we were able to gain the cooperation of authorities in both locations. However, we were at a dead end and needed a break in the investigation.

For the next several weeks, I stayed in Bangkok, reviewing reports and attending briefings regarding information supplied by other task force members who were following leads in Cambodia and Japan. Information developed produced credible evidence that the counterfeit notes were being produced in a country not accessible to US law enforcement and sponsored by that country's government. It was a state-sponsored counterfeiting of US dollars!

The focus of the source of the notes now shifted from Bangkok and Kuala Lumpur to that state sponsor of the criminal activity. Criminal investigations by US authorities inside that country would be impossible because of the closed nature of the state. Stopping the production of the notes now became a diplomatic or military issue.

That was above the pay grade of the task force members and would have to be worked out by the appropriate diplomatic leaders. The task force still operated and made substantial seizures of counterfeit currency throughout Southeast Asia but would never be able to get to the manufacturers of the currency as long as they remained within the confines of that country.

For me, my experience as a task force member was unique. I executed search warrants and interviewed suspects in foreign countries. I conducted briefings for foreign law enforcement officials and high-level US diplomats. I visited exotic locations and experienced different cultures. It was an experience that many US law enforcement officers never get to experience, and I feel fortunate Secret Service afforded me the opportunity.

EPILOGUE

O nce I left the New York field office, I spent five years at Secret Service headquarters and on the Vice Presidential Protective Division. Although I was away from New York and the criminal and undercover work I loved, I adapted to my new situation. I had great experiences with both Vice President Dan Quayle and Vice President Al Gore. I was on the detail for the 1992 presidential campaign and was part of the transition from the Bush-Quayle administration to the Clinton-Gore administration.

During both administrations, we traveled to some great places. We traveled to Cairo, Egypt, and had a personal tour of the Great Pyramid. We went on a safari in Namibia, Africa. We traveled to Pretoria, South Africa, for the swearing in of President Nelson Mandela. I was responsible for a protective advance to Jericho, a Palestinian territory, for a meeting between Vice President Al Gore and Yasser Arafat. I witnessed history firsthand during many of these trips.

We also traveled to numerous European cities, including Venice, Prague, Budapest, Warsaw, Bonn, Moscow, and St. Petersburg, to name a few. We traveled to South America to Bolivia, Argentina, and Brazil and to Africa to Nigeria, Benin, Ivory Coast, Malawi, and Morocco. I only did a few trips to Asia during my time on the detail. These included trips to Israel, Japan, and Almaty, Kazakhstan, where I was the lead advance agent for a meeting between Vice President

Gore and the president of Kazakhstan to discuss the nuclear disarmament of Kazakhstan.

Our first priority on these trips was always the security of the vice president and his family; however, during our time off, we were able to do some sightseeing and enjoy the local experiences. In Israel, I hired a driver, and we spent a full day touring the country. We explored the Old City in Jerusalem, Masada, Bethlehem, Nazareth, and the Sea of Galilee. We had lunch on the shore of the Sea of Galilee, where we ate St. Peter's fish. It was a truly remarkable trip and one of the benefits of being on assignment with Secret Service.

In Egypt, we rode camels and took a picture with the pyramids in the background. It was an awesome photo and one that hangs in my office to this day. All the travel and experiences were priceless and will be remembered for the rest of my life. Very few law enforcement positions afford the opportunity to travel and experience some of the things I experienced on a Secret Service protective detail.

During the first trip overseas for the new Clinton-Gore administration, we traveled to Warsaw, Poland. Many of the Gore staff members were young and inexperienced, and frankly, many had never traveled outside the United States.

Several agents, staff members, and I were in a pub in downtown Warsaw having dinner one evening. During dinner, at a table nearby, two men got into a loud argument. Both appeared to be drunk, and suddenly, one hit the other with a beer glass in the face. Blood splattered everywhere, and the men began punching each other.

A young staffer at our table jumped up and began to get between the men in an attempt to stop the fight, a very dangerous thing to do since other individuals were now involved in the fight and bottles were flying. I jumped up, grabbed the young staffer by the collar, and exited the pub with the rest of our party.

Outside, I read him the Riot Act. I told him it was a noble gesture to attempt to stop the fight but that he could have gotten seriously injured, and if the police came and we were involved, it would not look good for Secret Service or the vice president's office. The staffer acknowledged his mistake and thanked me. I attributed the whole incident to his inexperience and felt that he had learned a good lesson.

Well, that's a little bit about my experiences on a protective detail. I will save the rest of the story for another book.

My last day on the Vice Presidential Protective Division was on December 25, 1994. I was transferred to the Baltimore field office and was assigned as the group leader of the criminal squad. I was back to doing what I enjoyed most, working criminal cases.

As the group leader, I was second in charge of the criminal squad. I reviewed reports and supervised agents in the field. I worked less as a case agent and undercover agent and more as a supervisor and administrator. However, I did work a major undercover case, which I detailed in a previous chapter, while assigned to the Baltimore field office.

Much of the criminal activity in Baltimore at the time was credit card fraud and bank fraud perpetrated by individuals from West Africa. The crime was so prevalent that we started a West African task force and were able to have detectives from Baltimore City and Baltimore County permanently assigned to the task force.

We were working dozens of cases with substantial fraud and were executing several search and seizure warrants every week. Due to fraud thresholds of $100,000, many of these cases were not accepted for prosecution by federal prosecutors. However, with local detectives working the task force, we were able to prosecute many of these at the state level. Justice was ultimately served!

It was frustrating when federal prosecutors would not prosecute a case because it did not meet their threshold or would not get them in the headlines, but at least we found a way around it. In my opinion, many of the federal prosecutors did not want to get involved with fraud cases because they were complicated. They would rather prosecute a drug or gun case because many were not complicated and most defendants accepted a plea.

A good example of lack of prosecutorial zeal by federal prosecutors in Baltimore involved a counterfeiting case with a suspect from New York. A confidential source provided information that an individual from New York was in Baltimore attempting to sell a package of counterfeit currency. He stated he met this individual through an acquaintance and described him as a Dominican male about 250 lbs. and very tall. He stated that he would be able to contact his acquaintance and set up a purchase from the individual.

The confidential source placed a call from an undercover telephone line in the Baltimore field office to the residence of his acquaintance and connected with the individual from New York. The call was recorded by agents from the Baltimore office. The confidential source asked the individual if he could provide him with $10,000 in counterfeit, and he said he could.

The agreed-upon price was $1,500. A meeting was set up for 3:00 p.m. later that afternoon for the corner of Eastern Avenue and Ponca Street in Baltimore. The deal looked very promising. From my experiences in the New York office, I knew that Dominicans were expert counterfeiters; and since the purchase price was only 15 percent of face value, it indicated that the individual was close to the printer of the note.

Usually, the higher the price, the more removed from the printer the source would be. We might be able to work our way back to a counterfeiting plant, which was probably in New York. The confidential source was wired with a transmitter, and covering agents were sent to the vicinity of Eastern Avenue and Ponca Street. The covering agents identified the target's vehicle, which was a Chevrolet Camaro, waiting on the corner of Eastern Avenue and Ponca Street.

The case agent checked the confidential source's transmitter to make sure it was working and dropped him off several blocks from the target's location. The confidential source entered the target's vehicle, and after several minutes, he gave a prearranged signal to the covering agents through the transmitter, and the agents moved in to arrest the suspect and confidential source.

The $10,000 in counterfeit and the $1,500 in buy money were recovered, and both suspect and informant were transported to the Baltimore field office for processing. This deal was conducted on a Saturday, and the duty assistant US Attorney was contacted and notified of the arrest. As I stated previously, the Baltimore US Attorney had a lack of prosecutorial zeal for some cases, and this was one of those cases.

The duty assistant wanted to know why we had not contacted his office prior to the arrest even though we had clear probable cause to arrest and a substantial amount of counterfeit currency was seized. He stated that his office might not prosecute the suspect and that he would have to talk to his supervisors on Monday. I was livid, but it was getting late, and I told the agents on the scene that we would fight this battle on Monday. There was no way that they could not prosecute this case. It was cut-and-dried and an easy conviction.

Monday morning rolled around, and the case agent contacted the US Attorney and was advised that they would not prosecute the case. I called the supervisor and protested to no avail. We had to release the suspect. The suspect had just spent the weekend in jail, and by not prosecuting him, we were open to a civil lawsuit. To protect the agents involved, I had a plan.

I told the case agent to tell the suspect he was free to go but that he could not take his car because he was transporting counterfeit currency in it. We had a legal right to seize it. The case agent advised him that he would be contacted at a later date regarding the vehicle. The suspect was not happy about the vehicle but happy to be out of jail and left Maryland for New York.

I then contacted our Baltimore County task force officer and requested that he obtain a state arrest warrant for the suspect. Maryland actually had a statute regarding the possession, uttering, or sale of counterfeit currency, and that was the route we were going to go. Once the warrant was obtained, we would contact the subject and advise him that we would release his vehicle only to him; and when he arrived at the field office, the Baltimore County officer would arrest him on state charges. It was a great plan and worked like a charm!

A date was set for the suspect to pick up his vehicle, and when he showed up at the field office, he was met by the officer and three agents, myself included, and placed under arrest. We had four people because the suspect was six foot eight and about 260 pounds and didn't want to have an issue in the office. As you can imagine, the suspect was totally surprised when he was back in handcuffs but did not resist.

During the course of the investigation, we determined that the suspect was in this country illegally from the Dominican Republic, and immigration authorities were notified. The suspect appeared in the District Court of Maryland on the counterfeiting charges and was held on a detainer lodged by the Immigration and Naturalization Service. We made sure to do a press conference to let the US Attorney know that justice prevailed, and the arrest appeared in the *Baltimore Sun*. Ultimately, the suspect pled guilty to the state charges and was deported to the Dominican Republic. Justice was served despite federal prosecutors.

The last undercover deal I ever did occurred in Baltimore in the summer of 1997 while I was a supervisor at the Baltimore field office. My role as the undercover agent was requested by Secret Service headquarters. Normally, as a supervisor, you do not work in an undercover capacity, but headquarters felt I was the right person for the assignment. A confidential source advised that he knew of two individuals from Phoenix, Arizona, who were interested in purchasing a large amount of counterfeit currency. The Baltimore field office set in motion a reverse sting operation.

Arrangements were made for the confidential source to set up a meeting between me and the individuals in Baltimore's Little Italy. We obtained $500,000 in counterfeit currency involved in previous closed cases from Secret Service Headquarters to flash to the subjects. Hopefully, when they saw what I could provide, they would be ready to deal.

The meeting was set for Boccaccio's Restaurant on Eastern Avenue. The subjects flew into Baltimore and met me and the confidential source at the restaurant. Once we had a nice dinner, we planned to take the subjects to my vehicle and flash the $500,000 in counterfeit that was in the trunk.

Aside from the undercover agent getting hurt, the biggest fear in doing a deal like this was somehow losing the flash money. Having that amount of counterfeit stolen would be catastrophic. In addition to the embarrassment, the field office would be chasing those notes all over Baltimore for the next several years. To prevent this, a surveillance van with several heavily armed agents was set up in close proximity to my vehicle to guard it while I was in the restaurant and to protect me when I flashed the counterfeit.

The dinner was very cordial. Boccaccio's was an excellent restaurant, and the food and wine were top-shelf. Of course, I paid the $600 bill courtesy of the US government. As I later told my boss, "You have to spend money to make cases." In the eyes of the subjects, I looked like a high roller.

I advised the subjects that I had $500,000 in counterfeit currency and that I wanted twenty points, or $100,000 for it. They were receptive to that percentage but made no firm commitment to purchase. At the conclusion of dinner, I took the subjects outside and popped the trunk of my vehicle. Both their eyes opened wide when they saw the numerous stacks of counterfeit in the trunk. Both reached inside and began to rifle through it. I could tell that they were very impressed but still made no firm commitment to purchase the counterfeit.

The meeting was concluded with the understanding that the subjects would contact me in the next several days to discuss the deal further. I provided them with the undercover telephone line in the field office as my contact number, and I received a telephone number where I could contact them. I had contact with the individuals several times over the next few weeks; however, they still made no commitment to buy the counterfeit.

Our investigation revealed that both individuals were small-time criminals from the Phoenix area, and I began to doubt whether they could even come up with the $100,000 for the purchase. Several more attempts were made; however, the deal was never completed, and the case was closed. This case was not a notable, case but is mentioned because it was my last undercover deal.

I was promoted to assistant special agent in charge of the Baltimore field office in 1998. In this position, I was second in command for all Secret Service investigative and protective operations in most of the state of Maryland. There was a Baltimore supervisor who ran the criminal squad, so I had much less dealings with agents who were working the cases on the street. Although I missed the day-to-day criminal operations, the promotion to assistant special agent in charge was important because it was a progression to eventually becoming a special agent in charge of a field office.

During my time as a supervisor in Baltimore, I worked for three different special agents in charge. I had hoped to get promoted to that position in Baltimore; however, I had been there almost five years and felt that it was probably not going to happen. I spoke to the assistant director of investigations about it, and he advised that because of my five years in Baltimore, I would have to take a transfer to get promoted. Such was the Secret Service way.

My wife and family were very happy in Maryland, and I loved working in the Baltimore office; however, we made a decision to move. The promotion to special agent in charge was an increase in salary and would look good on my résumé once I decided to retire from Secret Service.

In late 1999, the Office of Investigations presented me with several choices for promotion. I decided on the Louisville, Kentucky, field office and started as special agent in charge in April 2000. My family stayed behind to finish school and joined me in June.

The Louisville office was a great place to work. The administrative staff was outstanding, and I had a group of young agents who were hard chargers. Louisville was a much smaller office with fifteen agents to cover the entire state; however, we were busy with criminal cases and protective visits. The year 2000 was a presidential campaign year, and we actually had the vice presidential debate in Danville, Kentucky.

To show support for the working agents, I would sometimes find myself out at night on a surveillance for a counterfeit or a fraud case. I wanted to let them know I was interested in what they were doing and appreciated all their hard work with the limited manpower we had. Additionally, it brought me back to the things I liked most about the job.

The 9/11 attacks occurred during my time in Louisville, and I could remember watching in amazement with the heads of the other federal agencies as the events unfolded on live television. Several agents in the field office volunteered to go to New York to help in the rescue effort.

Living in Kentucky was very nice, but we had a decision to make. My oldest son would be starting high school soon with the other children right behind him. I didn't want to move them when they were in high school, so if we stayed, we would be there for at least another ten years, and I would probably retire there.

My wife and I, both being from the East Coast, made the decision to move back to Maryland where our children had friends and where they could go back to the same great school they left. We actually moved back to the same community we moved away from.

In July 2002, through a friend who was a deputy assistant director in the office of the Protective Operations Division, I received a transfer to Washington, DC, as the special agent in charge of the Special Services Division. In this position, I was in charge of the armored limo program, the K-9 program, and the security force at all Secret Service facilities in the Washington, DC, area. It was an area of Secret Service that was alien to me, but I was glad to learn that aspect of the job and had great respect for the individuals who worked there.

After less than a year in Washington, DC, I felt that it was time to retire. My son would be attending a Catholic high school in the fall, which would be an added expense. My job prospects looked good, and I would be able to collect my pension. Financially, it made a lot of sense.

On April 3, 2003, I retired from the United States Secret Service after more than twenty years at a job I loved and felt privileged to have. On April 6, 2003, I started as a senior special agent with the Government Accountability Office, Office of Special Investigations. In this position, I conducted investigations for the US Congress regarding waste, fraud, and abuse within US government agencies.

About seven months after starting with the Government Accountability Office, I accepted a position with the Federal Air Marshal Service. The Federal Air Marshal Service was greatly expanded after 9/11, and many former experienced Secret Service agents helped expand the agency. I was assigned as assistant to the special agent in charge and supervised a squad of air marshals flying out of BWI Airport.

In 2007, I was promoted to assistant security director for law enforcement at BWI. I was responsible for federal law enforcement issues at BWI and for liaison with law enforcement partners and other stakeholders at the airport. In November 2008, I decided to retire from the Air Marshal Service after almost twenty-six years of federal law enforcement service.

Although I retired, I continued to work in the investigations and security field. I started my own private investigations company and conducted contract work for private corporations and government agencies. To this day, I work on an investigative contract for a major government agency. I plan on doing investigative work as long as I can. I love the work and love the challenge. I may have retired from Secret Service, but I will always be a street guy.

ABOUT THE AUTHOR

Thomas J. Farrell is a retired special agent in charge with the United States Secret Service. He spent over twenty years with the agency conducting and supervising undercover operations, criminal investigations, and protective operations. He became an expert undercover agent and was called upon to work undercover against members of the New York Mafia and transnational criminal organizations overseas.

Prior to his position with Secret Service, he was a police officer with the Waterfront Commission of New York Harbor. Upon retirement from Secret Service, he accepted a supervisory positions with the Government Accountability Office and subsequently the Federal Air Marshal Service. Upon retiring from the Federal Air Marshal Service, he started a private investigation and security consulting business. Currently, he conducts investigations for a federal law enforcement agency on a contractual basis.

CPSIA information can be obtained
at www.ICGtesting.com
Printed in the USA
LVHW091706170821
695505LV00006B/177

9 781638 810957